Guillotine

*To my wife Jean and
for my dear friend Gordon Anderson who kindly
shared with me his wealth of knowledge and picture
archives of the guillotine*

Guillotine

ROBERT FREDERICK OPIE

SUTTON PUBLISHING

This book was first pubished in 2003 by
Sutton Publishing Limited · Phoenix Mill
Thrupp · Stroud · Gloucestershire · GL5 2BU

This revised paperback edition first published in 2006

British Library Cataloguing in Publication Data
A catalogue record for this book is available from the British
Library.

ISBN 0 7509 4403 X

Typeset in 10/12.5pt Iowan.
Typesetting and origination by
Sutton Publishing Limited.
Printed and bound in Great Britain by
J.H. Haynes & Co. Ltd, Sparkford.

Contents

List of Illustrations   vii
Chronology   ix
Introduction   xi

1   Death upon the Guillotine   1

2   The Creation of the Guillotine   13

3   The Inventor and the Builder   29

4   A Simple Device   49

5   Terror   79

6   Justice and Retribution   93

7   The Cemetery   108

8   Dead or Alive?   120

9   The Guillotine and the Executioners   138

Epilogue   189

The Revolutionary Calendar   192
Appendix 1 The Pay of the Executioner   194
Appendix 2 The Executioners of Paris   196
Appendix 3 Locations of the Paris Guillotine   197
Appendix 4 Marie-Antoinette's Last Letter   199
Bibliography   202
Index   204

List of Illustrations

1.   The Halifax gibbet, used in Yorkshire in the sixteenth century.
2.   Guillotine, sent to Indo China (now Vietnam) early in the twentieth century.
3.   Dr Joseph-Ignace Guillotin, proposer of the 'simple device'.
4.   The Swiss guillotine.
5.   German Fallbeil.
6.   Queen Marie-Antoinette is guillotined at the Place de la Révolution.
7.   The heads of the Pollet gang.
8.   Louis XVI takes leave of his family before going to the guillotine.
9.   Waxwork image of Madame Tussaud, at the age of twenty-four.
10.   Anatole Deibler and his guillotine.
11.   Illustration of an execution from *La Police Illustrée*, 1883.
12.   'La Toilette du Condamné'. Illustration from *Le petit Parisien*, 1891.
13.   Käthe Kollwitz, *Die Carmagnole*, aquatint 1901.
14.   The execution of the 'Chauffeurs de la Drôme.
15.   The guillotine in Algeria.
16.   The executioner's hangar at 60 bis, rue de la Folie-Ragnault.
17.   Photo montage of a model guillotine.
18.   Older version of the German Fallbeil.
19.   An execution at Senegal in the nineteenth century.
20.   Executed criminal.
21.   Front view of the modern guillotine.

Guillotine

22.   The last public execution in France.
23.   Guillotine at Fresnes Prison in 1981.
24.   German Fallbeil and scaffold.

Chronology

1738 28 May: birth of Joseph-Ignace Guillotin
1757 François Damiens executed
1787 14 July: Dr Guillotin marries Marie-Louise Saugrain
1789 24 January: Estates General formally summoned by the
king
4 May–20 June: parliamentary convention to decide if it
should vote as a single body or as separate factions
17 June: the Third Estate (the people) adopts the new
title of the National Assembly
20 June: the Assembly proclaims the Tennis Court Oath
12 July: Tension and insurrection in Paris as Necker is
dismissed
14 July: The Bastille is stormed and falls to the mob
15 July: Necker is recalled to the Ministry of Finance
26 August: Declaration of the Rights of Man
5–6 October: the market women march to Versailles
9 October: reorganisation of the penal code proposed
2 November: the Church and its property are nationalised
1790 13 February: monastic vows are outlawed
1791 2 April: Mirabeau dies
20 June: royal family flees to Varennes
14 September: the king is forced to accept the new
constitution
1792 25 January: France and Austria are close to war
10 March: Dumouriez joins the government
3 March: Dr Louis devises the guillotine
15 April: the guillotine is tested on corpses
25 April: the appearance of the guillotine at the Place de
Grève

13 June: Prussia declares war on France
20 June: Tuileries Palace attacked by the mob
12 August: the Tuileries are stormed, and the Swiss guard killed
10 August: the monarchy is overthrown
2–6 September: September Massacres at the prisons
20 September: Dumouriez clinches the Battle of Valmy
22 September: France becomes a Republic

1793 16 January: Louis XVI is sentenced to death
21 January: the king is executed
1 February: war declared on Britain
March 1793–June 1794: the reign of Terror, 1st phase
2 June: the fall of the Girondins
10 July: Marat is assassinated
17 July: Charlotte Corday is guillotined
27 July: Robespierre joins the Committee of Public Safety
3 October: the Girondins sent for trial
9 October: Revolutionary Government is declared
16 October: Marie-Antoinette is guillotined
31 October: the Girondins are guillotined
8 November: Madame Roland is guillotined

1794 24 March: Hébertists are guillotined
5 April: Danton and Desmoulins are guillotined
8 June: the Festival of the Supreme Being
10 June–27 July: reign of Terror, 2nd phase
27–28 July: fall and execution of Robespierre

1795 6 May: Fouquier Tinville is guillotined

1814 Dr Guillotin dies

Introduction

This book explores the darker side of human inventiveness. It is a graphic and factual account of an implement of death which helped to create and dominate a culture that is uniquely French but of interest to all. Within these pages can be heard the echoes of the falling knife, levelling out a society and dealing with the criminal classes for the ultimate benefit of a new order. From its invention in revolutionary France until the last years of the twentieth century, this nightmarish machine has stood as the archetype of swift and merciful judicial death – but was it so? The facts are more complex.

The guillotine was perhaps the most notorious and fearsome method of execution employed in 'modern' times. The death sentence itself is an issue that continues to engage us. In the debate about justice and punishment the subject of judicial execution refuses to go away. This book is much more than a simple compilation of facts, weaving as it does a grotesquely interesting tale of a fearful implement used by society to oppress both the guilty and the innocent.

Guillotine, *n*. A machine which makes a Frenchman shrug his shoulders, with good reason.
Ambrose Bierce, *The Devil's Dictionary*, 1911

1

Death upon the Guillotine

For Claude Buffet and Roger Bontemps the last seconds of 27 November 1972 ebbed all too quickly into the new day. Condemned to death and held in the prison of La Santé in Paris, they were the main protagonists in a macabre drama that was yet to play its final act. At daybreak on 28 November justice required them both to meet the Grand High Executioner of the Republic of France – and the guillotine. Theirs would be the last executions by guillotine in Paris.

During a prison riot, Buffet and Bontemps attempted to escape from the Clairvaux prison. Buffet, already a convicted murderer, and his accomplice Roger Bontemps secured for themselves two hostages. Their bid for freedom was discovered but before they could be recaptured Buffet murdered both hostages, one of them a woman. Bontemps, now an accessory, found himself in the wrong place at the wrong time and with the wrong person. Though he had taken no part in the actual slayings, as Claude Buffet's accomplice he too was found guilty of the capital crime and would face the same fate.

* * *

'Peine de Mort' – 'Sentenced to Death'. The Tribunal's judgment on Buffet and Bontemps is spoken without emotion, remorse or regret; nor is it classed as some great judicial triumph of the Establishment. It simply marks the end of a trial where the punishment must be seen to fit the crime. This is how things are, or at least how they should be! It is a simple fact of life – and of death – that all judicial systems have minor flaws and all are flexible. Every crack can be explored and the system manipulated and twisted in any direction to save the lives of those condemned by it, but the lawyers must act expeditiously for there is no time for recriminations. An appeal against the sentence must be quickly formulated to defer their clients' fate and their early morning meeting with the executioner and the Timbers of Justice.

Perhaps some new fact may be discovered. Perhaps the conviction can be quashed on a technicality or because of irregularities. But no, not this time. The sentence is supported by public opinion and still stands. Time is fast running out for Buffet and Bontemps. All the evidence and the various controversies of the legal war waged within the courtroom have been pursued with vigour and commitment. The legal hierarchy's obligations to the statutes of France and its people have been fulfilled, and the guilty men, potential victims of state vengeance, have been removed from court and subsequently lodged within the sombre confines of the Santé prison. The final decision either to grant a reprieve or to send the men to their deaths upon the guillotine will be in the hands of the President of the Republic of France, after which there is no appeal.

The incumbent in 1972 was President Pompidou, a man of compassion, understanding and logic. He is painfully aware that he is the last hope for the condemned men. He understands well that technology in the form of the guillotine has outlived the humane philosophy of its revolutionary inventor. His own wish is to commute the dreadful fate that now awaits the living dead. The law is the law, however, and even the President must bow before the traditions, expectations and will of the French people.

Politics now interferes with his humanitarian and individual choices. Four times previously he has used his quasi-autocratic power to waive the death sentence. In this case, however, public opinion demands justice – and the heads of the two transgressors. The prisoners must prepare to meet their fate as determined by the unilateral voice and will of society. This is the will of the people. Individual instincts and moral compulsion may compel the President to reprieve the condemned, but the powerful cry for vengeance presses him to uphold the will of the people and their judgment upon the criminals. He upholds the sentence of death for Buffet and the unfortunate Bontemps.

The small time now remaining to the condemned men can be truly likened to a hell on earth. Given no indication of the specific time for their forthcoming execution, they can only wish for time to be suspended or confined to the bright daylight hours. Condemned prisoners can only relax on a few days: no executions are carried out on Sunday and Monday mornings or on national public holidays. The executioner does no 'work' on these days.

* * *

The imminence of death seems to draw the violent Claude Buffet into its tight grasp. Resigned to his fate, he even begins to welcome it. Ignoring the frantic efforts made by the defence lawyers to prevent his execution, he remarks, 'Tell everyone that Claude Buffet, the man that I am, wants to die on the guillotine. Let it be known that Claude Buffet commits suicide by the guillotine!' In contrast, Bontemps remains silent and impassive. Still hoping for reprieve, he is painfully aware of the nearness of his own death and can only wait out the little time that remains for him.

The prison director at La Santé will receive a communication from the office of the President confirming the sentence of death. At the same time the Executioner of the Fifth Republic also receives a notification of procedure. His reads:

Dear Sir,
In the Name of the Law,
Monsieur the Executioner of the High Works is hereby ordered to take possession of the individual named Claude Buffet, condemned to the punishment of death by the Assizes Court of Paris and to proceed with the execution within the confines of the prison of La Santé on 28 November 1972 at the legally established hour of daybreak.

An identical warrant is issued for Roger Bontemps. It is to be a double execution. The President has made up his mind, and the wheels of bureaucracy are trundling along to their inevitable conclusion.

The Chief Executioner must now make his own preparations. Without formality he sends a note to his valets (assistants). They will rendezvous at the Santé prior to the execution and quietly make their nocturnal preparations. Unknown to them all, they are passing an important milestone in the history of France: the denouement of the guillotine.

The unassembled guillotine is stored in an airy hangar within the Santé prison. The final assembly and adjustments will be silently carried out in the prison courtyard at the place of the Cour d'Honneur. Before the final assembly, a large black awning is erected over the courtyard to prevent any unauthorised watching of the 'National Razor' at work. The morbid machine seems to have become a taboo subject, shunned by authority. Is the guillotine an implement of justice that justice is ashamed of?

Inside the Santé the officers and wardens of the Quartier de Haute Surveillance continuously observe the condemned prisoners. Some offer succour and the encouragement of hope – always hope, but it is hope to the hopeless. Buffet and Bontemps each has a private cell and each is allowed certain liberties within the confines of the Quartier. They may smoke all they wish, send out personal correspondence, and receive visits from the prison chaplain and their legal representatives. They are no longer compulsorily restrained with leg irons or straitjackets, as was the case quite recently. Yes of course, there is still the chance of a reprieve. The President may yet commute the death sentence. The guards remain optimistic, until with a faltering voice the officer of the watch whispers to his company, 'It is for tomorrow – for certain.'

* * *

Just one week after the public execution of the mass murderer Eugène Weidmann at Versailles on 17 June 1939, the French government, disgusted at the behaviour of the rowdy crowds who flocked to witness such executions, passed a decree that all future executions within the city limits would take place privately in the confines of La Santé prison. This was intended to remove forever the public bloodlust aroused by the sight of the guillotine at work. Previously guillotinings had been carried out in public behind a police cordon, but it had become apparent that far from serving as a deterrent and having a salutary effect upon the crowds witnessing the feast of blood, this promoted the baser instincts of human nature and encouraged general rowdiness and bad behaviour. It was the taciturn victim of the blade who typically displayed the human dignity so lacking in the spectators.

The guillotine, robbed of its bloodthirsty and voyeuristic audience, was henceforth to be hidden from the public gaze, itself caged within the prison walls. It would become no more than a simple but efficient mechanical tool to carry out the wishes of the state on behalf of society. Nevertheless, whenever the guillotine was put to work, the execution still had to be witnessed by sane men. How strange that this act of judicial violence should have to be observed by normal peaceful men; one cannot help wondering whether they remained normal, untouched by the act.

The witnesses to the execution were designated by Article 26 of the Penal Code. This select audience comprised the following officials:

A judge of the Tribunal from the district where the execution was to take place and a clerk of the court
The presiding judge and a clerk of the trial assizes or a magistrate nominated by the first president
An officer of the public prosecutor's office
The chief of police and gendarme escort
The prison director of La Santé
The prison doctor or medical nominee
A minister of religion
The defence counsel

* * *

It was almost 3am when a call summoned the defence counsel to La Santé. Robert Badinter, abruptly woken from sleep and troubled dreams, now entered the living nightmare. Dressing hastily, he was brought along the quiet Parisian roads towards the prison. The rest of France would eventually awake to hear the news of the execution. Robert Badinter arrived at the prison and was taken towards the Quartier de Haute Surveillance. Entering the prison courtyard, he was confronted by his first sight of the guillotine, sometimes called 'the Widow' since all who lay with her were damned. It was fully prepared and waiting. The servants of the machine had expertly and silently completed their preparations and were nowhere to be seen; they had withdrawn to a room within the prison to await the arrival of the condemned.

An eerie silence prevails before the final ritual begins. In the dim light the machine seems almost alive, poised and waiting impatiently to embrace its fresh victims. Covered from prying eyes by the large black awning erected over the courtyard, it stands so very tall and slender, the distance between the uprights being no more than 14 inches. Its symmetrical bearing, although sinister and fearful, exerted an almost hypnotic influence over all who dared to study and observe it. Like a Medusa, it seemed to stare back with a narcotic power capable of turning the living observer to stone. Standing near the guillotine, one is in absolute awe of it.

It transfixed Robert Badinter's gaze and would not release him from its grasp. The compact base of the apparatus, though small to the eye, complemented the scale of the machine's malevolent and sadistic beauty. The *bascule* (tilting plank assembly) stood vertically and parallel with the uprights and seemed to point to the high nest where the gleaming blade, sharper than a sabre, lay in waiting. The heavy blade's weight was supported by a pincer-like device anchored to the crossbar holding tightly a spike that protruded from the *mouton* (the heavy weight that the blade is attached to).

The condemned men endure their uneasy sleep, troubled by hideous dreams, and unaware that the guillotine has been assembled and that the witnesses have already congregated within the Santé. The ever-vigilant prison officers suddenly stand to attention as the prison director appears; in response he simply gestures to his staff. There is no need for words; all those present anticipate the director's instructions. The strain lends a waxy pallor to their complexions, a pallor that is accentuated by the artificial lighting. The executioner and his assistants await the appearance of the condemned in a room close to the courtyard for the final '*toilette du condamné*'. It is then only a short walk to the guillotine. Without knowing why, Roger Bontemps is to be the first. The authorities deemed him to be the least guilty and to go first was considered a small act of mercy.

The wardens approaching the cell have slipped off their shoes. Even in the last few seconds they must not alert the prisoners, who are left undisturbed in their cells until the very last moment. Bontemps will be pounced upon before he realises what is happening. The door opens. The wardens enter rapidly, well drilled in the required manoeuvres. They firmly seize hold of Roger Bontemps. Sleepy and unaware, he is not sure whether what is happening is still a part of his dreams. His pulse quickens as he anxiously searches for a sympathetic face among the men around him, but there is nothing to comfort him or allay his worst fears; it is not a dream. The tension in his muscles gives way to a strange and strained acceptance of what is now inevitable. The final moment has come. The prison director stands before him and offers the traditional words: 'The President has rejected your appeal; be brave!'

Then Bontemps and his escort, preceded by the director, leave the dim cell; the ritual of the guillotine has now begun. Claude Buffet will follow shortly – the executions will be carried out consecutively. Strangely, there is no great hurry now. The bureaucratic wheels turn slowly, even before an execution; there are still formalities which have to be observed. The condemned move from room to room in turn. Each will be given back the clothes he wore on arrival at the prison and if they so desire they can take time to write a letter, perhaps to a loved one or a friend.

For each there will be Mass and Confession; finally they will stand before the director of the prison for the very last time. The director produces each man's prison record and signs it; the condemned man also signs it. Everything has now been officially and correctly carried out. The final statement on the record reads: 'Handed over to the Executioner of the High Works for carrying out of sentence.'

Like Pontius Pilate, the state has washed its hands of the condemned person. He has been given to the executioner, and is now his sole property. The *toilette du condamné* now follows. The hair is cut from the nape of the neck and the shirt collar removed with a large pair of scissors so that the shirt is left lying loose about the shoulders. The feel of the cold scissors on the back of the neck sends a shudder through the body, anticipating the feel of the guillotine's blade.

Robert Badinter has been very attentive, observing the hideous ritual as it slowly progresses through the prison precincts. They are now very close to the exit leading to the courtyard and death. It seems as if the victims of the state are taking part in a theatrical farce. They are offered large mugs of Cognac to help steady their nerves – the last human act before they enter the arena of death. Cords have already been cut to the appropriate lengths and are used to bind the arms and the feet. Badinter embraces Bontemps for the last time. Neither can speak. Emotion has overwhelmed them both, for what is there now to say but farewell? Is this ritual deliberately symbolic? A representation seemingly reminiscent of Christ's last moments before the cross as He was taken from staging post to staging post before the long climb to Golgotha? The symbolism is imprinted in Robert Badinter's mind.

Everything now seems to be ready. The prisoner, hampered by his leg cords, is assisted and supported by the executioner's assistants. They take him under the arms and speedily usher him into the courtyard towards the waiting guillotine. The witnesses, discreetly distant, follow at such a rapid pace that they seem to be almost running. Robert Badinter finds it hard to tell who is now the criminal and who the victim of this appalling night. The new killers, ashamed of their duties, wear a fixed expression, appearing to be masked as in a Greek tragedy.

As if in a trance Robert Badinter watches Bontemps's last moments. On reaching the guillotine, the valets directly behind him forcefully thrust him against the *bascule*. The weight of this living corpse falling on to the plank tips the mechanism down horizontally. The two assistants speedily push the *bascule* forward on its rollers into the jaws of the guillotine. Bontemps's head now lies on the lower block of the *lunette*, his neck between the uprights. The chief executioner pushes a lever, dropping and locking the heavy lunette in its closed position around the victim's neck. His ears are grasped and, like an animal in a slaughterhouse, his head is pulled forward in the *lunette*. A click is heard as the executioner pulls down the lever called the *manette*. The pincer device attached to the crossbar releases the blade assembly. In less than the blink of an eye it is down. The Widow has devoured her prey.

Robert Badinter heard the hollow sound made by metal sliding in metal, and the awful crashing sound as the heavy *mouton* and blade slammed home, the buffers at the base of the machine absorbing the impact. The blade slices with ease through the neck of Roger Bontemps. It has all happened in the space of a second. The decapitated head falls forcefully into a metal receptacle. The shuddering body, still bound by the cords, is thrown into a wicker body basket placed at the side of the apparatus. The bloody head, its eyes staring widely, is lifted from the receptacle by the ears and placed beside the body in the container. Both the panier and the body basket contain sawdust to absorb the blood. The executioner and his assistants, good workmen all, are throwing buckets of water over the housed blade and the courtyard. They wash their hands and arms clean of blood – so much blood! The guillotine is reset and all is again in readiness. The same horrific scenario is repeated and in half a minute or so Buffet is also dead. May Justice bless the guillotine and its servants for, according to the Law, Justice has prevailed. It is daylight now, and the Cour d'Honneur is empty; there remains no sign of the night's tragedy. The guillotine has been carefully dismantled and taken away to rejoin its sister machine. Satiated with the blood of many years, they rest quietly in the confines of an airy hangar.

* * *

Could any civilised and compassionate society look upon these events and not be repulsed by the sight, sounds and smell of such an ordeal? Was the continued use of the guillotine truly representative of justice and equality, or was there a better way? A new way to replace this sickening ritual, secretly and scurrilously carried out in the name of the law while all is cloaked in the anonymity of darkness?

After witnessing the deaths of his clients, Robert Badinter finally left the Santé prison. He too suffered at the hands of the guillotine and now bleeds with emotion from the wounds of trauma and despair, but it is in such great despair that the enlightened man can see something positive. Out of this terrible defeat he would grasp a distant victory and it would be his victory over the guillotine. He would fight fire with fire and adopt the mask of executioner, except that his target would be the guillotine itself. Along with other members of the legal profession, Robert Badinter would become a driving force behind the movement to lay the antiquated and barbaric machine in its own grave. It was a cause that Badinter took very seriously and which complemented his researches into justice in the revolutionary period and his wide-ranging interests in countering all forms of oppression and injustice.

How strange that the guillotine, an object of damnation, was created for all the right reasons: to put an end to the inequality of death prescribed by the state. To end the vile tortures, burnings and other pagan forms of execution, handed out and measured according to social class and status. The guillotine was the embodiment of equality in eighteenth-century France, but values change over time, sometimes for the better, sometimes not. In twentieth-century France revolutionary thinking is different, and its object must be the nobler hopes and aspirations of an enlightened people.

Agreement can never be unanimous on the punishment appropriate for certain terrible crimes. The 'National Razor' – one of the guillotine's many nicknames – has consumed the murderer, the parricide, the anarchist, those whose politics fell foul of the state and many others; and yet through successive generations they still remain with us. They will always remain with us, human nature being what it is. Perhaps a new way had to be found. Liberty, Equality, Fraternity – and now Enlightenment. Just as the guillotine was the product of an earlier, rather equivocal enlightenment, the machine itself now had to be abandoned – it had had its day.

The guillotine was never again used in Paris following the double execution of Bontemps and Buffet. The machine did have four further feasts in provincial France, the more graceful of the two remaining machines being used each time. The final execution took place at Marseilles in 1977, and the last victim, a sadistic murderer, asked for the forgiveness of France before his death. As it happened, he was not French but an impoverished and wretched immigrant, and France did not forgive him. Condemned to death on 25 February he was executed on the 10 September inside of Les Baumettes prison. Some would suggest, however, that now the guillotine was being used selectively and was even discriminatory in its choice of victims. An immigrant murderer of low social standing was far more likely to be executed than an equivalent French citizen from the higher echelons of society.

The issue of capital punishment, its morality and its deterrent value, always arouses strong emotion in debate. As a gross generalisation, though the opinion of the people may call for its return, it is unlikely that any political party in western Europe would ever reinstate it. Indeed such a reinstatement may even prove to be illegal within the ambit of authority of the European supreme courts. Throughout its lifetime the guillotine represented the ultimate method of ridding ourselves of our homicidal counterparts. Swift and mechanical, it proved to be extremely effective in dispatching even large numbers of those who were no longer wanted on the voyage! The trouble with the guillotine was that it was *too* efficient. It was loved and hated, loathed and admired. The love–hate relationship between society and the Timbers of Justice flourished; anyone who had seen the machine, provided it was not in use, could not help but be impressed by it. Its form, its lofty and geometric lines are pleasing to the eye. Its purpose, intentions and function exude a hypnotic power. The guillotine had style and was firmly entrenched in French culture.

By 1981 Robert Badinter had progressed in his career. He was filled with commitment and possessed the admirable quality of tenacity. In that year he became France's Minister of Justice and proposed a motion requesting the National Assembly to abolish the death penalty in France, thus completing the work begun in 1829 when Victor Hugo published his *Last Day of a Condemned Man*. The assembly and senate of the socialist government of France accepted the motion overwhelmingly. Badinter had triumphed, nine years after Roger Bontemps and Claude Buffet had been tipped into the abyss. After 188 years the rule of the guillotine was over, and the sound of its falling blade was silenced for ever. Vive la France!

2

The Creation of the Guillotine

In the calm before the storm, the *ancien régime* of France was apprehensive and disturbed. King Louis XVI and his wife Queen Marie-Antoinette may well have shared some of this disquiet, but were unaware of their destiny. They and many of their loved ones were doomed to die on a killing machine as the proletariat cheered and welcomed the affirmation of a new order.

Devised during the French Revolution, the guillotine, strangely enough, was not the product of vile or vengeful minds but rather was the idiosyncratic result of the egalitarian tendencies of learned men whose main concern lay in the notion of equality for all and the concept of man's humanity to man. The guillotine's insatiable appetite, driven on by the violent upheavals of a nation caught up in a radical change of direction, engineered its misuse. It could be argued that this assisted the growth of the modern ideology of man's inhumanity to man, since the machine continued to be used well into the twentieth century. Astonishingly, history shows that the number of deaths upon the guillotine in future years would far outnumber those during the revolutionary years in France, including the Reign of Terror. From its conception the guillotine was seen to be a highly efficient tool. Indeed, its sinister efficiency and sheer presence might even be thought to have created the demand for victims. A supply was duly obtained.

The French Revolution was eventually overtaken by the traumatic events it inspired and was subverted in its turn. In the outside world, its symbolic badge – the Timbers of Justice – lived on and prevailed. The Revolution in France liberated radical philosophical ideas, provoking strong debate and fiery oratory. This was the new platform for the politicians and thinkers of the day. 'Liberty, Equality and Fraternity' were to be the heralds of a new era, glorified by freedom of speech and the establishment of the rights of man; supported by the redistribution of wealth it was to redefine the role of the monarchy and the Church.

But the reality turned out to be rather different as the new breed of men fell foul of their own policies, hopelessly tangled in their philanthropic values and political beliefs. As Rouget de Lisle's *La Marseillaise* echoed through the political chambers, the many and various groups turned against one another. Jealousy, fear and intrigue were rife, and the secret police were kept busy; prisons were overflowing as the law caught in its web guilty and innocent alike. Underpinning all this was the fear of outside intervention as foreign powers watched and waited, like vultures round a wounded animal. Government degenerated into rule by denunciation, and instead of being protected by the law, individuals were greatly at risk from it: no one was safe. But at last, out of these turbulent times emerged the truly great and prosperous nation of France.

As the pace of the Revolution gained momentum, many of its gladiators were to perish, unable to hold on as the revolutionary wheel spun faster and faster, culminating in the Reign of Terror. The Revolution would eventually turn on the principal players and destroy them all with its Timbers of Justice: a king with no authority, a despised queen, Georges (Jacques) Danton the voice of the people, the unscrupulous Orléans, vain Bailly, those tigers of the revolutionary jungle Robespierre and St-Just, and thousands more.

At the heart of the political turbulence was the city of Paris, its people then near starvation, its politicians desperately trying to cope with unrest and revolt in provincial France and the escalating aggression elsewhere in Europe. Casting its long thin shadow over all was the inescapable spectre of the guillotine, the only certainty in France's turmoil. It encompassed royalty, aristocrats, politicians and peasants alike, beckoning them on with its blood-drenched arms. Out of the dramatic turbulence of the Revolution came the kind and philanthropic humanitarian Dr Joseph-Ignace Guillotin, whose reputation would be forever tainted by the infamous device that bore his name.

* * *

Joseph-Ignace Guillotin was born in Saintes on 28 May 1738, the ninth of twelve children. His birth (by popular conjecture) was premature, precipitated by his mother's chance witnessing of a distressing public execution. The penal code in the pre-guillotine era allowed for executions to be carried out by various methods according to the condemned man's place within the social hierarchy. For members of the aristocracy death might be painful but it was meant to be quick and relatively merciful. For the plebeian class it was something entirely different, often protracted, agonising and grotesque. Such hideous executions were not specific to French culture – they were endemic throughout the whole of the 'civilised' world. The penalty exacted by the state for capital offences had changed little over the centuries and feudal punishment was severe and often horrific. Before the victim received the *coup de grâce*, he or she was almost invariably tortured in the most barbaric fashion. This torture, known as 'the Question', was abolished by King Louis XVI not long before the Revolution.

The penal code of pre-revolutionary France listed more than one hundred capital offences, and criminals could be put to death in various ways. Beheading with a broadsword was reserved for the aristocracy, the skills of the executioner being of paramount importance. Any lack of expertise could result in a protracted and often cruel death. For the lower classes of society, the gallows waited. This effectively resulted in slow strangulation, perhaps lasting some fifteen or twenty minutes. (The neck-breaking techniques developed by the latter-day hangmen of England had not yet been invented.) The murderer, highwayman or bandit could expect to be broken on the wheel, an agonising death. A hefty bribe to the executioner might speed up the process but more often than not it was a long-drawn-out and hideous death. Religious heretics of the day, magicians and sorcerers were burned alive. The more merciful of the executioners would strangle the victim before the flames of the pyre began to burn the living flesh.

For an attack upon the king's majesty, would-be plotters and assassins faced a horrifying fate: they were hanged, drawn and quartered. The misguided regicide François Damiens (1714–57) made a somewhat ineffectual attack upon Louis XV with a penknife, which resulted in a scratch on the royal arm. Eight weeks of 'the Question' established that Damiens – a religious fanatic – had acted impulsively and alone. His assault upon the king was not part of any conspiracy aimed at destroying the monarchy. Stoically enduring the subsequent torture, Damiens was led from his internment within the Conciergerie prison, grey haired and almost insane. This pitiful remnant of humanity was to be put to death without mercy. He was to be taken to a place of execution, where, according to the court's judgment:

> on a scaffold that will be erected there, [Damiens's] flesh will be torn from his breast, arms, thighs and calves with red-hot pincers, his right hand, holding the knife with which he committed the said parricide, burnt with sulphur, and, on those places where the flesh will be torn away, poured molten lead, boiling oil, burning resin, wax and sulphur melted together and then his body drawn and quartered by four horses and his limbs and body consumed by fire, reduced to ashes and the ashes thrown to the wind. (*Pièces originales et procédures du procès fait à Robert-François Damiens*)

The executioner, perhaps ashamed of the cruelty meted out to the tragic Damiens, loosened the sinews and joints of his pathetic victim with a sharp knife so that he could be torn apart more easily. As darkness fell, mercifully masking the appalling scene of mutilation and death, the atrocious death of François Damiens, so reminiscent of the suffering of early Christian martyrs, was hidden from human sight – but not from history.

Some two to three hundred felons succumbed to execution in its various forms each year. It was Madame Guillotin's misfortune, on 27 May 1738, while in the late stages of pregnancy, to witness by sheer chance the screaming agonies of one of life's unfortunates who had been condemned to death by being broken on the wheel. The barbarity of the occasion made her collapse, and her ninth child, Joseph-Ignace, was somewhat prematurely ushered into the world the very next day.

* * *

The second half of the eighteenth century was an era of social upheaval and radical change. Science was blossoming and medicine was making giant strides. More dangerously, it was also a time of free thought and expression – a potent force and one that could prove lethal to a fossilised and entrenched government desperate to maintain the status quo. But for some of the most advanced thinkers, the greatest danger was to themselves and their disciples. When change occurs too quickly and freedom of speech is just too liberal, it can change and reshape the ideas and functions of society and thus promote anarchy. Those outspoken *philosophes* in the political sphere walked a tightrope over a very deep chasm into which they might fall at any time. Those incarcerated within the walls of the fortress called La Bastille could find no audience and any voices they heard were merely the echoes of their own. Charles Dickens characterised it with pinpoint accuracy: 'It was the best of times, it was the worst of times, it was the age of wisdom, it was the age of foolishness, it was the epoch of belief, it was the epoch of incredulity, it was the season of Light, it was the season of Darkness, it was the spring of hope, it was the winter of despair . . .'

The late François Damiens's moment of regicidal insanity

might have been inspired by – and so might compromise – the Jesuits and other religious factions, or better still those stalwarts of sedition, the *philosophes*. Such men, who believed passionately in change and progress, and who sought to undermine the monarchy, the aristocracy and the Church, made an easy and all-too-tempting target for the entrenched Establishment. Especially tempting were those who believed in equality of opportunity and the redistribution of the nation's wealth and power – perhaps the downfall of such men lay in the fact that they demanded too much change too fast. Many of the new thinkers secretly thought that some so-called offences against the state were not really crimes at all, and believed that France's ancient penal code, born of feudal superiority, should be modernised. Their plans for reform were all the more urgent because at any time the *philosophes* themselves might fall foul of the code's draconian punishments.

Brought prematurely into the world because of the effects upon his mother of the existing feudal penal code, Dr Joseph Guillotin would be the principal hand behind the restructuring of that code at the beginning of the Revolution. It was intended to bring justice in France up to date, but instead of being remembered as a humanitarian Dr Guillotin would be forever associated with the instrument of death called La Guillotine.

Joseph-Ignace Guillotin's father was a lawyer. He hoped that young Joseph, with suitable encouragement, would find satisfaction in theological studies. But Joseph soon forsook his Jesuit tutors and turned instead to the world of medicine. He progressed in his studies and by the age of twenty-three had received his diploma as Master of Arts. His medical studies earned him a prestigious award before he graduated at the age of thirty-two, after completing his thesis on the prevention of rabies. The interests and passions of Dr Guillotin were wide in scope and far-reaching. He was a stalwart member of the middle classes, and very much a patriot. As his career went from strength to strength he was appointed Doctor-Governor of the Paris Faculty of Medicine, in which post he published papers condemning the vinegar tax. He also put forward his ideas for draining the marshes of Poitou and Saintonge. Dr Guillotin was an extremely busy man, and the more work he did the more work he found; his energy seemed limitless.

Ignatius Loyola, the founder of the Jesuits, would doubtless have been proud of his protégé, steadily making progress in places that mattered. The good doctor became the guardian of the laws, history and traditions of the Masonic Order and was the much-respected Master of the Lodge of Paris Orient. He was also the orator to its provincial chamber. Dr Guillotin even found time to marry the beautiful Marie-Louise Saugrain on 14 July 1787, exactly two years to the day before the Revolution would begin in earnest. One year later, as the winds of change blew ever more fiercely over Paris and the approaching revolutionary storm gathered strength, Guillotin presented a paper to Parliament, the contents of which were dangerously controversial. Like Voltaire, whom he greatly admired as a defender of the oppressed, Guillotin presented a radical idea, precariously contending that the Third Estate, the people of France, should hold parliamentary supremacy over the combined voices of the aristocracy and the clergy. This may have been ambrosia to the patriotic inclinations and aspirations of the lower classes, but it left a very sour taste in the mouths of the old Establishment. Addressing such a petition to the king was a serious breach of protocol; worse than that, it was an unforgivable sin. But life in France was changing fast. Brought before the Convention to answer for his insubordinate petition, Dr Guillotin was vociferously supported by the people; though admonished, he left the hearing a free man, having been absolved by the first Civil Chamber.

At the age of fifty Dr Guillotin had become a public figure. The Third Estate would soon proclaim itself the National Assembly, marking the beginning of the end for the monarchy. The evolutionary process of political change was well under way, the ramifications of which would eventually be felt throughout the whole of Europe. Dr Guillotin was a pacifist and had no desire to weather the tempest of a bloody

Revolution. He was not alone. In the hearts of reasonable but far-sighted men lay the desire for an ideal new constitution achieved in a peaceful and democratic fashion. Such a constitution would retain the monarchy and conserve the accustomed prestige of the crown, but would also have democratic powers to suppress and curtail aristocratic privilege. There would be wise and fair government by enlightened and free men, not avaricious and incompetent aristocrats. Many such men looked across the Channel to England – the model of a democracy hard won by internal conflict but that still retained its (restored) monarchy. But England represented a dangerous precedent, for had not the English executed their king in former days?

* * *

In Paris, the continuing famine was undermining the morale of the city's inhabitants. A static and stagnating government, reluctant to change, was attacking the members of the States General which had convened on the 5 May. On 14 July 1789 the old ways were at last to be laid to rest in a sarcophagus of their own design. The powder keg that was Paris ignited and the popular call to arms was widely answered. The prison fortress of the Bastille, symbolic of all the wrongs done to France, was stormed and fell to the mob.

On 10 October 1789 the National Assembly, still resident at Versailles, had on its agenda the long-overdue reorganisation of justice and the penal code to take account of the notions of liberty and equality. Here at last was a subject that the erudite and industrious doctor–politician held dear to his heart – and it was to have far-reaching consequences. In such difficult times of political uncertainty it was imperative to bring about radical change to France's appalling legal legacy associated with crime and punishment. Expediency and the self-seeking interest of the new breed of men were also considerations, of course. The penal code listed sentences and punishments that through mere chance or poor judgement could fall upon anyone at any time, including the many members of the august National Assembly.

. Dr Guillotin was now an important man, a deputy of the National Assembly and a figure of significant political stature, and his proposals would no doubt attract the attention of his assembled peers. His ideas concerning the death penalty clearly had a nucleus of humanitarian reasoning at their core, but they were appropriate to the times in which he lived, and what was considered humanitarian then may be seen as almost barbaric today, particularly after two centuries of penal reform. It is interesting to note that at the same time as Dr Guillotin's proposals were being considered, the abolition of the death penalty was also proposed. However, such a far-sighted and profound idea was too advanced for the late eighteenth century. Indeed, for some civilised countries, even in the twenty-first century, the concept of abandoning capital punishment for certain crimes is preposterous. A host of considerations, including deterrence, reprisal, justice and tradition, have not been universally swept away by the onward march of reason and humanity.

Surprisingly, one of the main proponents of the abolition of capital punishment in the Assembly that day was Maximilien Robespierre, the delegate from Arras. Just five years later, as the savage director of the Reign of Terror, Robespierre himself met his end upon the Timbers of Justice.

Dr Guillotin put forward to an applauding and enthusiastic Assembly six articles re-evaluating crime and punishment; his plan was to create a new penal code, wherein justice and fair play would apply to all citizens, irrespective of rank or position. The doctor's proposals included the abandonment of all forms of torture, and the introduction of a 'simple device' to effect the quick decapitation of all criminals sentenced to death. The Assembly, much to the good doctor's chagrin, decided to adjourn for due deliberation before making its decision.

On 1 December 1789 the Assembly duly reconvened. The punctilious Dr Guillotin, still strongly motivated by humanitarian concerns, rose to his feet again and addressed the

Assembly. Determined to secure parliamentary agreement, he condemned feudal injustice and inequality and reiterated his six articles:

Article 1 All offences of the same kind will be punished by the same type of punishment irrespective of the rank or status of the guilty party.

Article 2 Whenever the Law imposes the death penalty, irrespective of the nature of the offence, the punishment shall be the same: decapitation, effected by means of a simple mechanism.

Article 3 The punishment of the guilty party shall not bring discredit upon or discrimination against his family.

Article 4 No one shall reproach a citizen with any punishment imposed on one of his relatives. Such offenders shall be publicly reprimanded by a judge.

Article 5 The condemned person's property shall not be confiscated.

Article 6 At the request of the family, the corpse of the executed man shall be returned to them for burial and no reference to the nature of death shall be registered.

Unfortunately for posterity, the doctor's speech to the Assembly was not recorded (or if it was, then it no longer exists). Suffice it to say that he condemned the old barbaric ways and discriminatory forms of punishment. It may be that he briefly described his 'simple mechanism', for he was quoted by a journalist describing its effect as saying, 'The mechanism falls like thunder – the head flies – the blood spurts – the man is no more.' (But no picture of his device exists).

Guillotin's proposals were in principle accepted by the Assembly but it adjourned again to reflect further on the implications of the new articles. Some people found it hard to accept that there should be no distinction between the death of a parricide, a homicide and a regicide. Article number one, however, was warmly received, equality being of paramount importance to everyone. It was clearly the desire of Dr Guillotin and his supporters that free Frenchmen should live with dignity and, if the time ever came, die with dignity in the name of Justice. The first article would ensure that this was so. Torture and inequality in death were no longer fashionable.

Within Dr Guillotin's six articles on the reformation of the penal code there was no detailed description of his proposed mechanical decapitator, only the brief remark that it should be a 'simple device'. To the doctor's surprise a malicious journalist, whose newspaper had clashed with Guillotin over a medical issue, seized the opportunity to denigrate the doctor and his ideas. This was the first sarcastic reference to the as-yet-unmade device: 'Should this execution device bear the name of Guillotin or Mirabeau?' The vulnerable doctor, always sensitive to the criticism of his peers, fell victim to sardonic mockery and innuendo. Libellous misquotes and verbal nonsense were attributed to him, and he was represented as saying: 'With my machine I'll cut off your head in a flash and you will feel nothing!' or 'The penalty I have invented is so gentle, that unless a man was expecting to die he would think only that he felt a slight breeze on the neck.' Perhaps he did say this or something similar, though it is more likely that an over-zealous reporter put the words into his mouth. The bizarre statements attributed to Guillotin gave a humorous tone to a very serious matter and are hardly in keeping with what we know of the good doctor's thoughtful and humanitarian character.

At the next meeting of the Assembly, Dr Guillotin donned the mantle of discretion and contributed nothing further to the debate. Perhaps he felt that he had made his point, or was reluctant to expose himself to further ridicule or laughter. His proposals would undoubtedly win through and be favourably accepted. It would just require a little patience; after all, even one day is a long time in politics! In any event, following further debate the Assembly passed three more of his proposals, to Dr Guillotin's silent satisfaction. However, the whole scheme still seemed to be in the balance, awaiting the outcome of the debate about execution by means of a decapitating machine.

When the Assembly reconvened on 3 June 1791 Dr Guillotin

preserved his somewhat melancholy silence and again pressed no further argument in support of his bill. The Assembly's favourable response continued with the approval of a further article and finally accepted that 'Every person condemned to death shall have his head severed' ('*Tout condamné à mort aura la tête tranchée*'). On 20 March 1792, nearly three years after Dr Guillotin's proposals had been presented to the Assembly, his articles became law. Without further ado or debate it was also recommended that: 'Decapitation should be by means of a machine.' Charles-Henri Sanson, then the public executioner, had made representations to government suggesting that manual decapitation might actually lead to numerous accidents. Too many things could go wrong with this notoriously unreliable means of execution. A machine was the answer, conducting the decapitation of the condemned in a humane and impartial manner.

The sombre but triumphant doctor sat back with an air of satisfaction, knowing that he was the man mainly responsible for bringing the true concept of equality to the penal code. But his sense of satisfaction was fleeting, for the 'simple device' was all too soon to stain his good name with the blood of its victims. The contraption he had merely proposed would bear his name forever, leaving behind a grisly legacy.

Dr Guillotin's brainchild was born at the right time, but in the wrong circumstances. Revolutionary France was already spiralling out of control and plunging forward into the Reign of Terror, an era that the machine itself would make possible. Once over the threshold of the realm of chaos, the falling blade of the guillotine would begin its relentless march of death. Popular belief has credited Dr Guillotin as the designer and inventor of the machine but in fact he was neither. He may have had a basic idea about the type of machine suitable for the purpose and perhaps even discussed the merits of such a device. If he ever referred to the decapitator as 'my device', which is questionable, he would have been referring only to the *type* of device he thought was most suitable. There is nothing on record to show that he ever submitted a plan or a design for a decapitation machine. He had no need or desire to abandon his medical and political role to become an inventor. In any case, it simply was not necessary for him to do so, as such a machine already existed, albeit in a much less sophisticated form. Another common misconception about Dr Guillotin is that he perished beneath the blade of his device during the French Revolution. This is not true, and he lived into a ripe old age.

* * *

It is worthwhile recalling two anecdotes that have been linked to Dr Guillotin's inspiration to make the 'simple device'. On one occasion the doctor was going about his business in Paris when he happened to observe the ongoing construction of a bridge. In order to hammer home the supports of the structure, the industrious workmen used an early form of manual pile-driver. The connection becomes instantly obvious. The heavy weight of the hammer was repeatedly hauled aloft before being released to drop on to the bridge's timber supports, driving them into the ground. It was a very simple device indeed – and it only needs a large blade to be added at the base of the weight and a prototype decapitator is conceived. The second story relates to the doctor's presence with his wife at a Parisian fair where they watched a pantomime entitled 'Les Quatres Fils Aymon'. The act included a staged execution carried out by means of a primitive beheading apparatus in which an axe slid down between two upright poles. Could Dr Guillotin really have been inspired by these or similar observations? It seems unlikely.

More than one hundred years before the Revolution in France, a certain marshal named Henri de Montmorency was beheaded at Toulouse by means of a primitive machine. The execution took place in 1632 and was described by one Jacques Chastenet. A *doloire* (a type of carpenter's axe) was held between two timber uprights by means of a rope; when the rope was released the axe descended and severed the head from the body. It is often assumed that the French were the originators of mechanised decapitation, but this is erroneous. A very early woodcut in the British Museum shows that the Irish were the first to dispose of their condemned criminals by means of a rudimentary form of decapitator. The victim is shown kneeling on a scaffold with his head on a timber block, being consoled by monks. The executioner is cutting through a rope beneath which a heavy straight-edged blade is suspended. Though the style of dress worn by the participants may look distinctly Elizabethan, the text indicates that the apparatus was used to behead Mercod Ballagh on 1 April 1307. In Italy during the pre-guillotine age the 'Mannaia' was used to decapitate the gentry. In some German states the primitive-looking 'Diele' was utilised to hack off the heads of men and women irrespective of social status. In England the 'Halifax Gibbet' was used for the occasional decapitation of felons and is reputed to date back to the post-Norman invasion era.

None of these primitive head-chopping artefacts has survived for closer inspection, but in Edinburgh can be seen 'the Maiden' – the precursor of the guillotine. The word maiden is thought to derive from the Celtic phrase *mod-dun*, referring to a place where justice was administered. The device was introduced into Scotland from England sometime during the sixteenth century and its design was probably based upon the Halifax Gibbet. As already stated, the Halifax Gibbet probably originated in the period after the Norman conquest of England and it was certainly in existence – and use – in the reign of King Edward III (1327–77). James Douglas, Count Morton, installed the Maiden in Scotland. Ironically he was beheaded by means of the device in 1581 after being found guilty of high treason.

The Maiden comprised two oak pillars just over 3m tall and spaced 31cm apart. At the base of the uprights was a block set 92cm from the ground. A cross-rail joins the pillars at the top and at the ground. Each pillar is supported at its outside and the whole contraption is maintained in the vertical position by a large timber support running from the top cross-rail to the ground at the back. The horizontal blade that slides up and down between the uprights is 33cm in height and 27cm wide, and is capped by an iron block weighing 35kg. A hinged iron bar holds the victim's head securely upon the block. Without doubt it was a true fore-runner of the guillotine.

All these devices may appear to be similar to the guillotine, but they differ considerably in technical specification, overall speed and efficiency. The rudimentary head-choppers were all fitted with horizontal straight-edged blades. There was generally no device to immobilise the head of the victim properly, and the body was never secured to the apparatus to enable a swift and efficient execution even if the condemned was struggling. The straight edge of the axe bludgeoned the neck in a crushing fashion, hacking off the head, and if accidents occurred the results would have been horrific.

When the guillotine was eventually constructed and tested, it was equipped with a sloping-edged blade that struck the neck at an angle of 45 degrees. The victim was strapped to a tilting plank called the *bascule*, thereby immobilising him at the base of the machine. The head and neck were also securely held between the uprights by the *lunette* (literally 'the little moon'). The upper section of the *lunette* could be moved up and down within a groove running parallel with the grooves that held the blade attached to its heavy weight or *mouton*. When the blade of the guillotine was released, it fell and struck the neck obliquely, slicing off the head instead of hacking it. The guillotine was without doubt a modern and efficient killing machine that in skilled hands was able to dispatch its victims quickly, at a rate of about one a minute. There was nothing crude or basic about the guillotine. Nothing like it had been seen before, and with its eye-catching and almost hypnotic qualities it soon established itself as a part of French culture, remaining functional for more than a century and a half.

It is obvious that Dr Guillotin was never required to rack his brains over the concept of a mechanical device to serve the requirements of justice. Pantomimes and pile-drivers may have given him the idea, but the prototypes of the guillotine were already to hand. The requirement was simply to bring a little eighteenth-century technology to bear upon existing models and to modernise them accordingly. Dr Guillotin's high-minded principles were at last to blossom into reality. He would henceforth be known as the man who mitigated the inequality of judicial death that had prevailed for hundreds of years. There was to be no more slow strangulation by hanging from the gibbet, no more burnings, no more brutal and agonising deaths upon the wheel and no more torture. All of these forms of state retribution that had prevailed even during the early period of the Revolution would soon be gone. Any future delay in the practice of good execution and equality for all would not be due to a lack of will but more the result of the slow progress made by the wheels of bureaucracy and the inertia of the National Assembly.

On 25 March 1792, in the eighteenth year of the reign of King Louis XVI, the law relating to the death penalty and the mode of execution was at last modernised. The king was no doubt in agreement with the higher humanitarian values that had precipitated such change, for it was he who had originally abolished the awful procedure of 'the Question'. For King Louis, however, his eighteenth year of autocracy was to be his last. He had unknowingly become responsible for his own future demise, thanks to a simple mechanical device and a doctor's good intentions.

Dr Guillotin slowly bowed out of the political arena, taking a less prominent role in the affairs of the Assembly. The political climate was to become intolerable as revolutionary tigers and extremists began to hold sway over events. The Revolution gathered momentum, propelling it forwards into the Terror. Soon all would be overshadowed by the lofty form of *les bois de justice*, the guillotine.

3

The Inventor and the Builder

With the acceptance of the revised penal code in its entirety the construction of the guillotine became a matter of urgency. Worries had already surfaced concerning the efficacy of the new law. The simple beheading of all condemned prisoners may have satisfied the egalitarian principles of those concerned with the administration of the law, but the practical problems posed had not been addressed. Very practical considerations engaged those who were required to perform the actual deed.

The dignified behaviour of a condemned aristocrat, whose qualities of breeding, bearing and fortitude matched the dignity of the occasion, could not be expected from the common people. Thus the use of the traditional sword to execute a number of condemned persons of varying degrees of courage and temperament would certainly be a cause for concern. After all, the law, though often severe, should never be cruel.

Charles-Henri Sanson, Executioner of the High Works ('maître des basses et hautes oeuvre') was a man of considerable experience. He was required to submit a memorandum on execution to the Justice Department and for Dr Guillotin's attention. The contents of the memorandum pointed out the impracticality of applying the new law without having the right tools for the job. It was a disappointment to some members of the Assembly and more particularly to the judiciary that M. Sanson's observations did nothing to speed up the construction of the guillotine in time to coincide with the practical application of the new code.

The memorandum affords an insight into the character of the man who served as the state's executioner throughout the Revolution. His appointment was ratified by the monarch – whom Sanson duly executed. Without prejudice he then went on to execute on behalf of the revolutionary moderates the extremists who had condemned the king. He was a man of considerable expertise, devoted to his somewhat unsavoury vocation and very talented in the art of self-preservation. The memorandum reads:

Memorandum from the Executioner of the High Works, Charles-Henri Sanson.

In order that an execution may be completed according to the requirements of the law, it requires that, without any hindrance on the part of the condemned man, the executioner be very skilful and the condemned very composed, otherwise it may be impossible to complete the execution by the sword without the risk of dangerous incidents occurring.

After each execution the sword is unfit to perform another; it is essential that the sword which is liable to damage be sharpened and reset if there are several condemned persons to be executed at the same time. It is therefore necessary to have a number of swords available in a state of readiness.

It will be noted that swords are very often broken at such executions. The Paris executioner has only two swords, presented by the former Paris Parliament. It must be considered that when there are several condemned to be executed on the same occasion the terror presented by the execution due to the great quantities of blood flowing in all directions will horrify and weaken the bravest of those still to be executed (and those who have to carry out the execution). Such weaknesses may turn the execution into a struggle and a massacre.

As a result I have to give warning as to the accidents that may occur if such executions are carried out by use of the sword. It is essential in order to satisfy the humane opinions of the National Assembly that means be devised to immobilise the condemned man to ensure the execution and make it a matter of certainty. The law would be fulfilled and one protected from public outcry.

Sanson's memorandum confirmed that the construction of the guillotine was of paramount importance in order to conform with the spirit of the law and the Assembly's desire for equality. Indeed, the absence of the new machine was considered unforgivable by those whose job it was to administer justice. The various sections of the National Assembly, already inept and confused, now seemed to be caught up in endless bureaucratic mayhem, resulting in a general lack of drive and commitment in getting the whole issue off the ground. Finally an exasperated Department of Paris Directoire felt compelled to approach the President of the Assembly concerning the delays. The importance of the situation was illustrated by the case of one Nicolas-Jacques Pelletier, a condemned felon found guilty of robbery with violence and assault with a knife. This veritable French Dick Turpin should have been executed ten weeks previously, but his execution had had to be postponed owing to the Assembly's lethargic approach and inability to produce the right tool for the job. The authorities were all quite aware that the new law stipulated capital punishment must be by decapitation using a machine, but the machine did not exist! Sanson the executioner, who doubtless could have performed the task adequately with a sword, was unwilling to do so. This was now modern France, and to use such a crude method might lead to unintentional cruelty. In the executioner's opinion such an act would undermine the spirit of the new law and incur a loss of public confidence. Sanson's statement reamplified his earlier memorandum; he clearly felt that it was his duty to fulfil his function as humanely as possible.

The Minister of Justice, M. Duport-Dutertre, was already under pressure from his colleagues to act quickly, and he too felt compelled to raise this urgent matter with the President:

I am obliged to submit for the urgent attention of the National Assembly a point requiring an immediate decision. I reluctantly speak of the requirement to carry out the judgments of the courts, and in the interests of humanity the importance of not arousing the adverse ferocity of public opinion. I make reference to the means of execution. The new code indicates that sentence of death should only involve the deprivation of life and nothing else. Since decapitation is the penalty that conforms with this principle, a form of execution must be sought which, made uniform, will meet the requirement.

Duport-Dutertre, Minister of Justice, 3 March 1792

Dutertre never knew that he too would perish beneath the blade a year later on 29 November 1793.

The National Assembly was finally motivated to engage itself with the matter, and to this end enlisted the expert aid of Dr Antoine Louis, permanent secretary to the Academy of Surgeons and an acquaintance of Dr Guillotin. Dr Louis was requested to report with all speed on the manufacture of a suitable machine to serve justice as swiftly and painlessly as possible.

At sixty-nine years of age, Dr Louis was another humanitarian. Many eminent republicans could be listed among his friends, and by profession he would prove to be the ideal candidate for the task in hand. Already the innovator of many surgical instruments, now he was to produce a scalpel of rather unusual proportions. This rather cynical but gregarious character measured up to the challenge splendidly and on 17 March 1792 submitted his detailed report to the Assembly. His report is of some importance since it gives the primary description of the first guillotine, the machine that would truly hold sway over the heads of the people of France.

Method of Decapitation – A Reasoned Opinion

The Legislative Committee has done me the honour of consulting me on the subject of two letters written to the

National Assembly, concerning the implementation of Article 3 under Division 1 of the Penal Code which states that 'Every person condemned to death shall be decapitated.'

From these letters the Minister of Justice and the Department of Paris Directoire, in view of the representations made to them, judge that there is an urgent need to precisely determine the method by which the law should be carried out. There is a fear that the execution through some defect in the means employed or lack of experience or unskilfulness would become horrific both for the condemned and the spectators. The people, moved by feelings of humanity, may then behave cruelly and unjustly towards the executioner, a situation which is important to avoid.

In my opinion the representations are fair and the fears well founded. Experience and reason indicate that the method hitherto used in beheading a criminal exposes him to punishment more terrifying than the mere deprivation of life which is the explicit desire of the law: to fulfil this wish the execution must be performed instantaneously and with a single stroke. There are many examples to show how difficult this is to achieve.

We can recall the facts observed at the execution of M. de Lally when he was beheaded; he was kneeling with his eyes bandaged; the executioner struck him on the neck; the head was not severed. The body, with nothing to prevent it falling, fell forward and only after three or four blows of the sword was the head severed from the body. This 'hatcherie' – if I may invent the word – this hacking to pieces was witnessed with horror.

In Germany the executioners have more experience due to the frequency of this sort of execution, mainly because persons of the female sex no matter what their social standing are subjected to no other form of execution. However, the perfect execution may still not be achieved despite the precaution in certain places of seating the victim in a chair.

Guillotine

In Denmark there are two positions and two instruments used in decapitation. The form of execution that may be described as honourable is carried out with a sword; the criminal kneels with his eyes covered and his hands are free. If the execution is to convey ignominy, the criminal is bound, laid face down and his head cut off with an axe.

Everyone should be aware that cutting instruments have little or no effect when they strike perpendicularly. If studied under a microscope it can be observed that they are more or less fine saws which only work by sliding them over the object to be cut. It would not be possible to behead a person at a single stroke with a hatchet or axe of which the edge is straight, but with a convex edge as on the old battle-axes the blow is not perpendicular except in the middle part of the axe. The implement, as it penetrates more deeply into the substance it is dividing, has an oblique sawing motion at the sides and therefore attains its function with certainty.

When we consider the structure of the neck, of which the centre is the spinal column, it is composed of several bones which overlap in such a manner that no joint can be located. It is not possible to be assured of a prompt and perfect separation when the task is entrusted to an agent whose skill is variable owing to moral or physical reasons. To ensure certainty in the proceedings it should depend upon non-variable mechanical means whose force and effect can be determined. This is the view that has been adopted in England. The criminal is laid face down between two posts joined by a crossbeam at the top from which a convex axe is made to fall on the neck by means of a trigger. The top of the instrument should be sufficiently strong and heavy to act effectively like a ram that is used for sinking piles; it is known that its force increases proportionately according to the height from which it falls.

It is easy to have a machine of this kind constructed and its effect unfailing: the decapitation will be accomplished instantaneously in accord with the spirit and intention of the new law; experiments can easily be carried out on corpses or even living sheep. It can be determined whether the head of the criminal should be held in place by a crescent-shaped cross-piece which will encircle the neck at the base of the skull; the top or projections of this crescent could be fastened by pins under the scaffold. This apparatus, should it be necessary, would not be felt and would hardly be perceptible.

Paris, 7 March 1792
Louis, Permanent Secretary, Academy of Surgery

Dr Antoine Louis's extremely prompt reply was a reflection of his professional nature. He sprang into action with the vigour of a man half his age, and with a mind as keen as the edge of the guillotine's blade set to work devising a specification for a prototype of Dr Guillotin's grand idea. It is not known whether Louis and Guillotin discussed the design of the machine. It is curious that Dr Louis's letter to the Assembly included references to pile-drivers and to the Halifax Gibbet, which he obviously believed was the standard tool for dispatching English felons. It seems odd that a man of his standing and experience should not know that the gallows was the principal method of execution in Britain.

So, Dr Guillotin had proposed the adoption of a 'simple device' and Dr Louis had theoretically almost invented it. All that was required was to find someone to build it. Dr Guillotin could not endure the thought that his name might be associated with a killing machine. His anxiety was lifted when Dr Louis appeared on the scene at the planning stage. The Academy's permanent secretary became so enthusiastic about the project that Guillotin's involvement seemed to be eclipsed and soon the inventive powers of the media prematurely baptised the new device 'Louisette', much to Guillotin's relief and Louis's chagrin. Dr Louis's sensibilities were just as vulnerable as Guillotin's. He attacked his cynical critics and perceived enemies, accusing them of obscenities. He, like Dr Guillotin, saw himself as a humanitarian and told a friend about his dislike of those acrimonious journalists who were only too willing to defile his good name and intentions. Later on, Dr Louis was to insist that he was not the inventor of the guillotine, but that at a late stage in its development he had been instrumental in correcting the shape of the blade to enable it to cut cleanly and achieve its objective. Thus he threw all the blame back on to poor Dr Guillotin. Both men indignantly protested their 'innocence', but it was Dr Louis who 'won' the battle. His name has faded into obscurity while Dr Guillotin will be forever linked with the guillotine.

Dr Louis duly prepared and submitted his specification for the device. On 23 March 1792 the first guillotine began slowly to materialise. The Procureur Général M. Roederer contacted the Minister of Taxes, M. Clavière, to ensure the necessary measures were being taken to allow the prompt construction of the new machine. The minister passed the information to the Directory of Paris, requiring that he should be kept informed of the estimated costs involved in its manufacture. Typically Dr Louis had already completed the groundwork as the estimate was submitted for scrutiny. Nicolas-Jacques Pelletier, it seemed, would not be kept waiting much longer for his appointment with death. The carpenters' estimate for the cost of the machine was prepared by M. Guedon, who at the time supplied Paris with its execution gibbets. Guedon's figure of 5,660 livres was widely considered to be exorbitant, but the high costs involved were the result of Dr Louis's detailed technical specification. This gave the first detailed description of the constructed guillotine:

1. Two parallel upright posts of best-quality new wood (new chestnut), actually the French guillotines were all eventually constructed of oak, five and one half metres high joined at the summit by a crosspiece. This frame to be firmly erected upon a base with supports at the side and rear. The uprights are to be 15cm in thickness and placed 30cm apart. On the inner side of each upright will be cut longitudinal square grooves 3cm deep to take the side pieces of a blade. Beneath

the crossbar at the top of the uprights there will be secured a brass pulley.

2. A high-quality well-tempered blade will cut on account of its shape being convex. The cutting edge will be 17cm wide and 15cm high. The top of the blade will have the thickness of an axe. The blade will have at its top fixings to attach a heavy weight of 15kg or more. The ram will be furnished with an iron ring on the middle top part. The blade-holder will measure 30cm across, with two square tenons projecting 2cm at the sides. The blade-holder must be able to slide down the grooves of the uprights.

3. A sufficiently strong and long rope will be threaded through the ring of the knife-holder and will maintain this under the upper crossbar. The rope will pass over the pulley from the inside and will be fastened on the outside at the foot of the uprights.

4. A wooden block on which the victim's neck will rest will be 20cm high and 10cm thick. Its width will be the distance between the two uprights. The block will be held between the two uprights by detachable bolts. The block should be assembled so that it is not cut by the fall of the blade. The top of the block should be scooped out to comfortably lodge the victim's neck.

5. To secure the head so that it is not lifted at the moment of execution, an iron crescent like a horseshoe should encircle the neck at the base of the skull where the scalp ends. The extremity of the crescent reasonably extended should be pierced to allow it to be held in place by a bolt passing through the upper part of the block.

The victim lies face down, his neck resting on the scooped-out portion of the block. The executioner will be able to hold the two ends of the rope supporting the blade-holder, and by releasing them at the same time the instrument, falling down from a height, will by its mass and acceleration separate the head from the body in the twinkling of an eye. Errors within the specification can easily be rectified by even an elementary builder!

Guillotine

M. Guedon was not an elementary builder. Did Dr Louis's acid and unnecessary comment touch a nerve with the master builder Guedon, upon whose carpentry skills depended the prompt manufacture of what was now an essential piece of equipment? The specification did not even describe the mechanism for releasing the blade; certainly it would take more than an elementary builder to construct this eagerly awaited device. The high costs involved in the manufacture of the new death machine were justified by M. Guedon in the resumé of expenses he submitted. Of course it went without saying that the work would have to be carried out in a professional manner commensurate with the skills of a master craftsman. M. Guedon's estimate was as follows:

1. Initially, the professional carpentry of the machine
   and the scaffold upon which it will stand   1,500 livres
2. For the stairway of the scaffold and its supports   200 livres
3. For the required iron fittings   600 livres
4. For three trenchers   300 livres
5. For pulleys and copper grooves   300 livres
6. For trials, time, vacations and meetings relative
   to the construction   1,200 livres
7. For the model to be used to avoid as much as
   possible subsequent errors and to prove the
   efficiency of the full-scale machine   1,200 livres
8. For the ropes   60 livres
   Sum total   5,660 livres

M. Guedon soon became aware that his quotation was viewed unfavourably by Dr Louis and the members of the Establishment, and he felt it necessary to offer some justification as to the costs involved in producing the first example. Perhaps he was anxious lest the government agency should view his quotation as greedy and unpatriotic, the more so because the machine was a government contract and public necessity. To vindicate and defend the costs of his quotation he argued as follows: 'If the costs involved appear somewhat expensive, it should be noted that any further machines built on the pattern of the initial model would be much less expensive, all of the difficulties being overcome as regards estimated costs and modifications should there be a need for them.' He also pointed out that some prejudice and difficulties would have to be overcome in locating tradesmen willing to work on the manufacture of such a shocking device, even if it were in the interests of humanity. Such prejudicial behaviour, however, does sound somewhat unlikely, as there was never any objection to making a new set of gallows.

Guedon probably felt insulted that he should be categorised as an elementary builder by a supercilious surgeon, the same doctor whose activities would shortly culminate in the grotesque and ghoulish behaviour of cutting off the heads of corpses. Clearly there was a degree of animosity between the inventor and the potential builder, but it seems that Dr Louis may have had an ulterior motive in antagonising M. Guedon.

The Procureur Général M. Roederer had received the estimate for the construction of the guillotine and forwarded it to Clavière on 5 April 1792. Accompanying the estimate was a letter of his own. Initially Roederer accepted the quotation and was quite happy to recommend its acceptance to Clavière. But the belligerent Dr Louis would have none of it. Having cast doubt on the honest nature of the unfortunate Guedon, he recalled a certain acquaintance, a maker of harpsichords and inventor. He would be the ideal person to build his machine.

Roederer's letter to Clavière read:

Monsieur,

Dr Louis has forwarded to me an estimate from Master Guedon, carpenter, supplier of gibbets, for building the machine designed to behead criminals; I have the honour to send you a copy together with the letter from the secretary of the Academy of Surgeons, who though approving the ideas does not conceal the fact that the costs appear to him to be exorbitant. I cannot refrain from making the same comments myself. One of the reasons on which Master Guedon bases his demands is the difficulty of finding workers for tasks which by prejudice may shock them. This prejudice does in fact exist, but workers have offered their services to construct the machine at a far lower cost than his, providing their names are not made public. In the event of your rejecting the estimate I have forwarded, it would be right that you authorise the Directory to deal with some other tradesman.

Roederer.

On 9 April Clavière acknowledged the communication. He wholeheartedly agreed with the contents; he was after all the Minister of Finance. The estimate was scandalously expensive; another builder must be approached, and soon. M. Roederer, who took his duties very seriously, was now being pestered by numerous functionaries to get something done and fast. The courts, realising that the results of their judgments were not being acted upon, were becoming impatient with the bureaucratic sloths who seemed unable to produce the guillotine. The exhausted Roederer was now under considerable pressure. Just days before sending his letter to Clavière he had met again with Dr Louis, Dr Guillotin and several other luminaries from the medical profession. Also present at the gathering were Dr Lacuée and Dr Broussonnet, Master Guedon and Charles-Henri Sanson, the Paris executioner. Was it at this clandestine meeting that Guedon, in spite of the opinions of Dr Louis and Roederer, refused to reassess his costs for the manufacture of the machine? Elementary builder indeed!

Meanwhile, Pelletier was still waiting in the condemned cell, much to the consternation of Judge Moreau of the Second Paris Tribunal, who wrote a letter of complaint to M. Roederer:

The machine has not yet been constructed while in prison there is an unfortunate man condemned to death, who realises his fate and for whom each moment that prolongs his life must be a death for him. In the name of the law and humanity, in the name of the service which our courts endeavour to render, be so good as to give orders to terminate the causes of the delay, which damages the law, public morale, the Judges and the culprits themselves.

Pelletier himself, who was to provide the first sacrifice on the new altar, was not at all dismayed by the postponement of his death. He had already waited months and would have preferred it if the busybodies representing justice had taken a little less interest in his welfare and excluded him from their bickerings.

Stung by Judge Moreau's fulminations, M. Roederer immediately replied to the letter – and it was not at all promising for Pelletier: 'Since yesterday, M. Louis and another have been working on the machine and have promised it for Saturday; a test can take place the following day using a corpse and on Monday or Tuesday the sentence on Pelletier can be carried out.'

The 'other' individual working on the machine was one Tobias Schmidt. Dr Louis and Procureur Roederer found him the perfect technician to assist them in their haste to have the guillotine built and operational. Schmidt resided in the Commerce-St-André, close to where Georges Danton and Camille Desmoulins lived. A German by birth, he manufactured harpsichords and pianos, and was also a self-appointed inventor. He was not unknown to the National Assembly. At various times he had submitted to it a range of inventions, all of which were to the benefit of humanity. There was a hydraulic diving apparatus complete with communications system, a fire escape ladder, an easy-to-pull plough and a pianoforte that could imitate the sounds of the violin, the bass and alto. Schmidt even used his talents to design his own mechanical decapitator, but the design was impracticable and it was never adopted. He was also reputed to have sold musical instruments to the executioner Charles-Henri Sanson, who enjoyed nothing better in his moments of relaxation than to play the violin. Their unusual friendship may have accounted for Schmidt's interest in the mechanical decapitation process.

One can almost imagine Sanson and Schmidt playing duets in the executioner's residence and in their conversational breaks discussing the merits and perplexities of the design of an instrument that played no tune at all. Could Schmidt have been overtaken by enthusiasm and so produced his ideas for such a device? A design was certainly submitted to the authorities in the person of M. Laquiante, commissaire to the king. Was Louis XVI first made acquainted with the concept of the machine through this channel? Did this later prompt the king's curiosity and his suggestion concerning the shape of the blade in a story penned by Alexandre Dumas in his work *The Tragedies of 1793* (see page 46).

Once his own design was turned down, Schmidt turned his attention to Dr Louis's saturnine creation. Dr Louis must have been delighted with the enthusiasm of his new technician and, even better, Schmidt had assured Roederer of his own sense of duty and fair play in the matter. There would be no inflated prices or robbing the public purse for Schmidt. The cost of producing Dr Louis's device would be 960 livres, and the price would even include a leather bag for the disposal of the severed head, referred to with typical French humour as the 'family picnic basket'. On 10 April 1792, charged with energy and a rather disturbing devotion to the task in hand, Dr Louis reported to the Procureur Roederer: 'The inventor of musical instruments is now busy by your command with an instrument having quite a different purpose!' Evidently he had not lost his sense of humour, even under duress. The undercut M. Guedon, purveyor of gibbets, was not completely excluded by the often inebriated German. For the sum already quoted, he was retained to construct the heavy-duty scaffold upon which the machine would stand.

* * *

Bicêtre, an establishment not far from Paris, was used primarily as a prison and public hospital. As an added bonus for the community, the facility also housed old and homeless members of society who could find no other shelter in revolutionary France. In April 1792 it must have been a most interesting place for a casual observer. The chief surgeon of Bicêtre Hospital was Dr Michael Cullerier, a bachelor and humanitarian. As a member of the medical profession Dr Louis trusted him implicitly and could depend upon his support and cooperation. It was 12 April 1792, and the construction of the first guillotine had been completed, probably in the vicinity of M. Schmidt's workshops at the Place St André des Arts. Dr Louis communicated with his colleague Dr Cullerier concerning the trials necessary to prove the efficiency of his new device. He wrote:

> Monsieur, the engineer authorised to construct the machine will be ready to try it out on Tuesday the 15th April. I have informed the Procureur Général so that he may give instructions to the person required to operate it in public to be present on Tuesday at 10 o'clock at the site planned for the tests. I have also informed the Directoire of the Department of your zeal and cooperation. For the fall of the blade to be effective the machine must be at least four and one half metres high.
>
> Louis

Dr Cullerier's zeal and fullest cooperation reflected the widespread interest among Louis's medical peers in the challenging task of producing the guillotine. It also became apparent that Dr Cullerier, in the interests of science, would be only too happy to provide a plentiful supply of cadavers for experimentation. Business-like, prompt and polite, he responded to Louis's letter:

> Monsieur Louis,
> At Bicêtre all facilities will be available to carry out the tests of the machine which humanity cannot contemplate without a shudder but which justice and society's welfare make a necessity. I shall retain the corpses of such unfortunates as may die between now and Monday. The theatre shall be

arranged in a suitable manner. Should the ceiling prove too low for the height of the machine, a small and private courtyard may be used which is located beside the theatre. Sir, your choice of the hospital of Bicêtre I consider an honour. It would be even more so if you would consent to dine with me and accept the simple and frugal meal which a bachelor can offer you.

The 'unfortunates' were, of course, not asked whether they were willing to participate in the trials and thus contribute to the greater good of society.

On 15 April 1792 the congregation gathered at Bicêtre to witness the official testing of the 'simple device', already assembled in the courtyard. But this was not the very first test of the celebrated instrument of modern justice. Earlier that month the new machine had been erected in the courtyard that served M. Guedon's workshops. Dr Louis himself was absent from this dry run but he was represented by a young and curious acolyte, Dr Nysten. As there were no corpses available, two sheep and two calves had been obtained from a local abattoir. It was assumed that the necks of these twice-condemned herbivores would present the same degree of resistance to the fall of the blade as a human neck. The heads of the unfortunate animals were duly sliced off to the satisfaction of the team without any problems. However, testing the new machine on animals was all very well but it was not enough for Dr Louis. The true test of the apparatus was to be carried out in the little courtyard at Bicêtre.

Those present at Bicêtre to witness the first official trial run of the 'petit louison' included Dr Louis and Dr Guillotin. The honourable host was Dr Michael Cullerier. Other guests representing the medical fraternity included doctors Cabanis, Lacratelle, Maret, Nysten and Philip Pinal. Charles-Henri Sanson and two of his brothers or assistants attended in their professional capacity to offer advice. Sanson had been kept abreast of the development of the machine commensurate with his post as Executioner of the High Works.

The Inventor and the Builder

Dr Cullerier, as promised, supplied a number of fresh corpses for the machine's private debut. It has been suggested that some journalists and other invited guests were also present, making a grand total of approximately fifty people. In one small courtyard? It seems unlikely. Newspaper editors of the day would have ensured the reporting of any sensational story or event, but the guillotine's debut received little attention. The tests would certainly have been of interest to everyone since the new machine had been devised for the benefit of humanity at large. The press would hardly let go unnoticed the fact that a condemned man's future lot was now greatly improved, even though the end result would be the same!

The assembly of the guillotine was supervised by Tobias Schmidt, carefully observed by Sanson and his aides, who arranged three (or perhaps five) corpses. The guillotine then went into action. To the unbridled delight of the observers, the falling blade sliced off the first bloodless head with ease. Sanson was more than impressed by the guillotine's efficiency, saying: 'It is a fine machine – as long as its facility is not abused.' He would soon find out just how efficient the machine could be. One of the busiest men employed by the revolutionary government, he would cut off more than 1,500 heads in just one year, including those of the king and queen of France.

But as the witnesses began to congratulate Dr Louis on his success, it all went drastically wrong. The head of the next corpse, a muscular male of large proportions, was not cleanly decapitated but remained partially attached to its torso by strands of cartilage and sinew. There was unanimous agreement that death would anyway have been instant, had the victim been alive, but nevertheless the notion of partly severed heads was as unacceptable to the team as it would be to the public. Disappointed and despondent, the team had little appetite for the frugal lunch prepared by the gracious Dr Cullerier.

Clearly there was an inherent fault in the design of the machine. This would have to be addressed immediately and proved by further testing. They could not risk such a thing happening at a real execution. Three possible modifications could be made. The height of the uprights could be increased to accelerate the blade even more; the *mouton* – the sliding weight that held the blade in place – could be increased in weight; or the shape of the blade could be changed. Time was of the essence, and remedial action had to be taken quickly to identify and correct the fault.

Dr Louis and Dr Guillotin this time put their own heads to good use! Taking into account the acceleration and force of the falling axe, they concluded that the fault must lie in the design of the blade. Instead of the original convex shape, they chose to install an oblique blade.

* * *

For those who enjoy the ironies of life there is a story concerning the shape of the blade which is worth recalling. It is found in Alexandre Dumas's work *The Tragedies of 1793*:

At the third try, the crescent-shaped blade of the guillotine had only done three-quarters of its job. Let us relate how the modification which led to the perfection of this instrument of death, and which distinguishes it today, came about. King Louis XVI heard about the trial which had taken place in the courtyard of Bicêtre Hospital and the displeasure shown by Dr Guillotin could not be hidden from him.

The King, as everyone knows, was a good mechanic and above all a very skilled locksmith. The first time he had a chance of meeting Dr Louis he had the mechanism of the machine explained to him. Dr Louis took a pen and made a rough sketch of the instrument.

The King examined the drawing carefully and when he came to the blade said: 'The fault lies there, instead of being shaped as a crescent, the blade should be triangular in form and cut obliquely like a saw.' To illustrate his words Louis XVI took a pen and drew the instrument as he perceived it. Nine months later the head of the unhappy Louis XVI fell beneath the instrument which he himself had designed.

The Inventor and the Builder

A similar story was told by Clément-Henri Sanson, the grandson of Charles-Henri Sanson. Clément was the last of the Sanson dynasty of executioners and recalled the tale from his grandfather's notes and memoirs. A fanciful story told to a journalist, it echoes the version of events written by Dumas. In Sanson's tale, the king has a meeting, incognito, with doctors Louis and Guillotin. Charles-Henri Sanson, the Executioner of the High Works, is also in attendance. The machine is again described to his majesty who, with a keen eye for anything mechanical, suggests to Sanson that the device has an inherent fault. The king recommended that the shape of the blade be made triangular. 'Such a blade would therefore be able to accommodate all necks!' said the king.

* * *

Undeterred by the failure of the initial Bicêtre tests, Dr Guillotin and Tobias Schmidt returned to Paris and quickly commissioned a new and redesigned blade. Its new form was the great oblique-edged knife that is still recognised as the benchmark of the guillotine.

Another test was arranged at the Bicêtre Hospital, when Dr Cullerier once again provided appropriate corpses – large muscular men only recently deceased. This time when the blade came crashing down, the skin, muscles and vertebrae of each corpse yielded easily to the all-powerful blade of the guillotine, or, as Carlyle described it, that great Cyclopean axe.

The involvement of Dr Guillotin with his simple device ended with the successful experiment at Bicêtre. After all was said and done, he still had no wish to have his own name linked to such a dreadful implement. He refused to witness a single execution carried out in the new fashion. He found it intolerable when the term 'guillotine' was mentioned in his presence and strongly protested against the sinister apparatus being named after him, but by now no one paid him any heed.

Dr Louis too tried to disassociate himself from his invention. He became embarrassingly sensitive at the prospect of his name being associated with a death machine. He was not even present during the final and successful test. His sense of humour, so resilient previously, seemed to give way to shame. It upset and annoyed him whenever the infernal device was labelled 'La Louisette' or 'Le Louison'. When anyone referred to 'his' machine he would point out angrily that the credit should be given to Tobias Schmidt's ingenuity for the appearance of 'les bois de justice'. In fact, it was due to Dr Louis's own dedication and persistence concerning the project that the guillotine would soon be stretching out its arms to welcome all and sundry. It was Dr Guillotin's great misfortune that his name was forever associated with the device. There is no doubt that the true creator of this fearful implement was old Dr Louis, permanent secretary to the Academy of Surgeons. At 69 years old, he died from pleurisy in the same year that the guillotine was created, 1792, but some still believe it was from shame and grief that his name, as he thought, had been given to an instrument of death.

4

A Simple Device

The Hôtel de Ville stands in the Place de Grève. Typical of Paris, the Place de Grève is surrounded by architecturally outstanding buildings, close to the soft currents of the River Seine; it is a most pleasant place to be on a warm April afternoon. The crowds gathered there excitedly to watch the first execution with the new device. No one knew what it looked like or how it functioned. The atmosphere was one of anticipation, the crowd jovial and friendly, motivated in no small part by curiosity. The guillotine, now thoroughly tried and tested, was ready at last to make its impact felt and to imprint itself on the pages of history. It was to begin its bloody career in earnest, a career that would eventually span almost two centuries, far outliving its creators and their children's children. The uniquely French machine would outlive the Revolution and further advances in penal reform. As a device of deterrence and correction, it would soon travel the world.

In the days that preceded its arrival at the Grève for its official debut it had undergone some cosmetic changes and was now painted in a startling bright red finish, mounted upon a high and imposing scaffold. The guillotine was a machine that any executioner could be proud of! The forthcoming execution of Nicolas-Jacques Pelletier, who still had not been forgotten by the Second Criminal Tribunal of Paris, was scheduled to take place on 25 April 1792. The unique circumstances of the occasion – the guillotine's inaugural use on a live criminal – gave rise to some concern over the issue of public safety and the safety of the new implement.

Guillotine

M. Guedon, now the purveyor of scaffolds instead of gibbets, had been engaged to supply a sufficiently strong and reinforced platform that would safely support the guillotine and absorb the wave of energy as the blade slammed down and rebounded on impact. The dreadful noise of the double crash would soon become all too familiar to the crowds that regularly gathered about the scaffold at the various sites where the machine was operated. Even people too far away to observe the guillotine in use would hear that loud double crash as another soul was sacrificed on the Revolution's high altar of equality.

M. Roederer, the Procureur Général, who was as efficient and far-sighted a man as could be, was aware that a large crowd would assemble for the event and took care to ensure that all would go well on that auspicious day. The novelty of the new spectacle would guarantee a splendid day out for the crowd, while the ignorant and apprehensive Pelletier had no concept at all of what was going to happen to him. All he knew was that he was to be the day's entertainment, playing out his last moments before a live and vociferous audience. M. Roederer wrote a letter to M. Lafayette of the Garde Nationale. Lafayette himself would survive the forthcoming Terror but his life was deeply affected by the consecutive executions of those whom he loved most dearly.

To M. Lafayette, General of the National Guard
Monsieur,
The new method of execution will undoubtedly attract large crowds to the Grève and we must ensure adequate steps are taken to avoid damage done to the new machine. It is necessary for you to order the gendarmes who will be present (commanded by Captain Fortin) at the execution to remain in the square and its exits to facilitate removal of the machine and scaffold.

Three days before the execution was to take place, the newspapers carried lively editorials advising their readers that

A Simple Device

'An experiment – the new method of execution is to be tried out for the first time!' An updated report read:

> The machine invented for beheading criminals condemned to death is to be used today (25 April). The machine has several advantages over the methods previously used. It will be less revolting and no man's hand will be stained by the slaughtering of his fellow man. The condemned will endure nothing but the apprehension of death which will be more painful to him than the actual blow which robs him of life.
>
> To test the effect of the new device, Nicolas-Jacques Pelletier, convicted by verdict without appeal on 24 January 1792 by the Third Provisional Criminal Court, is to be executed for the crime of theft and attempted murder. The Tribunal has sentenced him to be taken to the Place de Grève dressed in a red shirt and there beheaded in accordance with the provisions of the Penal Code. (Uusually the wearing of a red shirt was reserved for parricides.)

How very fair and easy it all sounded; a man's death had become almost trivial. The wretched Pelletier should have been quite reassured by it all, but he was not. As the journalist suggested, the expectation of death, however quick and merciful, weighs more heavily upon the conscious thoughts of the condemned than does the actual moment of passing. It is not the dying, but the fear of certain and premeditated death that causes anguish.

Pelletier went to the scaffold with none of the courageous indifference displayed by many of the guillotine's later aristocratic victims. His behaviour vindicated Sanson's views about the difficulty of beheading a victim manually if he was distressed or lacked the moral fibre to die with dignity. Sanson's memoirs relate how Pelletier was carried up to the scaffold and strapped to the *bascule* while in a fainting fit. Perhaps the horror of the unknown eroded the little courage that Pelletier had left. It was doubtless small compensation to his family that he was the first man to die in accordance with the high-minded principles of the state, soon to be the First

Republic of France. The guillotine had taken a little over two hours to assemble and erect; after Pelletier's appearance at the machine the execution took only a minute.

Sanson, who was accustomed to be the chief player in public executions, now seemed to pale into insignificance beside the new scaffold. Under the old laws, he was instrumental in playing the role of the terrifying '*bourreau*', not only to the victim but also to the audience. Now he played a much less obtrusive part, his only action being the elementary act of releasing a latch. Sanson, the grand master, did not have to lay a single finger upon that first unfortunate victim.

Robbed of the eagerly awaited cruelty and spectacle of a traditional execution, the expectant crowd's jubilation and gaiety were instantly subdued by this new way of killing. Those who blinked momentarily, or were engaged in conversation at the fatal moment, missed everything. It seemed as though the whole drama was over almost before it had begun, such was the speed of the guillotine. For the crowds that had assembled, it was a complete disappointment. Pelletier's corpse was not even available for viewing; all that could be seen was the blood-soaked machine.

The art of executions and making an example of the condemned had entered a new phase. The suspense of the victims, miserably waiting for their final agonies to begin, no longer entertained the watching crowds. The guillotine was to introduce a new mode of death, quick and egalitarian, designed to reform a degenerate society of feudal and antiquated habits. The new breed of audience would no longer have the chance to contemplate the vicious and prolonged suffering of the poor condemned. Such primitive spectacles had been abolished at a single stroke and the visual presence of death changed forever. The astonished crowd stared at the guillotine with uneasy displeasure. If the machine had been a living entity, with eyes to see, it would have looked back at the people in anticipation as a cat would watch a mouse. The guillotine had been truly baptised in blood and was seemingly now alive. But this speedy, almost clinical, death by machine was not what the crowds wanted. The ritual of the good death, the public confession, the shocking but somehow salutary display of physical violence – all these had been swept away. It would take some time and many deaths for the guillotine to establish itself as a great social spectacle, a cleansing and necessary ritual of Revolution.

* * *

Was the machine that dispatched Pelletier so efficiently the same as that tested within the Bicêtre Hospital? It probably was, and the authorities no doubt viewed its first use as a great success. It supported all the high-minded principles of the Revolution – liberty, equality and fraternity. If a quick and reputedly painless death could be a criterion of liberalism, then it satisfied the test. Egalitarian it most certainly was, since all who were condemned to perish had meted out to them an equal punishment. Fraternity was also upheld, since no human hand was laid upon the deadly blade. Yes, as was demonstrated on a warm and pleasant April afternoon in 1792, things had definitely improved, but it would be at a cost.

The newspaper *Chronique de Paris* reported the reaction of the crowds after the execution. The public were not impressed, though it would not take long for the spectacle of the guillotine to increase in popularity. According to the *Chronicle*:

The people were not satisfied at all. There was nothing to be seen. Everything happened too fast. They dispersed with disappointment, consoling themselves for their disillusionment by singing,
Give me back my wooden gallows
Give me back my gallows

The disappointment of the people would soon change as a widespread euphoria began to manifest itself. Unknown by its inventors, the guillotine had cleared the way for a revolutionary tempest. A machine created by philanthropic and humanitarian men of the highest motives had made its entry into history at a time when the storms of revolution were gathering momentum.

Three days after the execution of Pelletier the machine was in action again. Three soldiers were condemned to death after they had murdered a poor street vendor, a man who spent his days selling lemonade. Since they had killed a civilian, justice was meted out by the civil courts and not by the military. Messrs Devitre, Debrosses and Cachard duly climbed the steep steps of the high scaffold where the Widow's embrace awaited them. Subsequently three forgers were executed. Then on the 3 July 1792, the first woman, Anne Leclerc was guillotined. The next execution in Paris occurred on 21 August and claimed it's very first political victim. Louis-David Collenot d'Angremont, administrator of the National Guard. The guillotine was swiftly moved to the Place du Carrousel, where the crime was said to have taken place, there to be used as an instrument of exemplary public punishment in front of a large crowd.

Dr Louis and Dr Guillotin both played vital roles in the creation of the guillotine but neither wished to be associated by name with the device, especially after it had caught hold in the public imagination. The guillotine became a female entity. Its very name was the feminine form of its proposer's name, and it was also colloquially known as the 'Widow'. It also had a number of other nicknames: it was the National Razor, the Patriotic Shortener, the People's Avenger and Lady Guillotine. It even achieved dubious immortality as Sainte Guillotine. As far as officialdom was concerned, the term guillotine was seldom used. It was not a death machine but an implement of justice known as the Timbers of Justice. In later years even members of the criminal class adopted a sort of masochistic admiration for the implement. The life-and-death relationship between crime and punishment was painfully real, but they lightened the mood by having the words 'Cut along the dotted line' tattooed around their necks.

As the public became more captivated by the guillotine, it seems rather ironic that no individual wanted to claim at least a share of the credit for its production. Dr Louis, desperately trying to shrug off the responsibility for his invention on to other shoulders, graciously presented the honour to Tobias Schmidt: 'Indeed,' stated Louis in a letter to M. Roederer, 'Sieur Schmidt is the ingenious inventor!' Tobias Schmidt had no such worries concerning authorship of the omnipotent device. Nothing suited his schemes better than to have his name inexorably linked to the machine. His enthusiasm for the project even tempted him to try to take out a patent for the guillotine in his own name, very much to M. Roederer's annoyance. Roederer was later to say of him: 'He is not in reality the inventor . . . he only made a few alterations to Dr Louis's description.'

Poor Dr Louis! He could not escape the responsibility for producing the guillotine, no matter how hard he tried. Schmidt, of course, was motivated by money. With so many districts now demanding their own guillotines in order to fulfil their obligations under the revised law, many new machines would have to be constructed, all at great cost. To Schmidt the guillotines represented a very lucrative proposition indeed, not to mention the profitable supply of spare parts to keep them functioning.

On 5 June 1792 M. Roederer, busying himself in his accustomed fashion, asked the architect M. Giraud to submit a report on the performance and technical specification of the machine. Sadly for Schmidt the report was a damning indictment of his incompetence and dubious carpentry skills, and he was soon to find himself in the alarming position of a lost sheep among bureaucratic wolves. M. Giraud's critical report also attacked Schmidt's costs:

Although the implement is well conceived, it has not been perfected to the fullest possible extent to ensure the public's peace of mind. The grooves, tongues and gudgeons of the implement are in wood. The grooves should be made of brass, the others of iron. Hooks to which are attached the ropes holding up the weight (mouton) are only secured with nails and should be fixed with strong nuts and bolts. A step is required to the plank (bascule). Straps are too low, insufficiently strong and too open. Also two moutons and blades should be kept in reserve as replacements in the event of an accident occurring. I have also been assured that this particular machine can with its improvements be manufactured for a total of 500 livres.

Five hundred livres! The integrity of Tobias Schmidt was under attack, along with his shoddy device. It had to be a mistake: a skilled artisan like Schmidt, who could manufacture musical instruments, was being virtually accused of having fleeced a government department. But if there was anything shoddy going on, then it was in that subversive and stinging report. Even M. Guedon's estimate for the machine minus the scaffold had been 1,500 livres. The avaricious and undercutting Schmidt, friend of Dr Louis and acquaintance of Sanson, had promised it for 920 livres. No complaints were heard then about these bargain basement prices, but 500 livres was nothing less than preposterous. Schmidt wondered who could possibly supply the machine for such a price. It turned out that the man in question was one M. Clairin, who operated his small business near the Théâtre Français, and was a friend of the architect M. Giraud! For Tobias Schmidt, the report was deeply wounding. Was there no integrity left in the world?

Schmidt endeavoured to reconcile the problems mounting up around him, but failed. His popularity with the various Departments and particularly with M. Roederer had traumatically – and very unfairly – waned. Here was a man of talent who was quite happy, unlike Dr Louis, to be recognised as the machine's parent. Not only that, but he had also applied for a patent on the implement's design. Schmidt had nothing to hide and nothing to be ashamed of, or so he thought.

By the beginning of May he had already begun work producing more guillotines. Two had been completed for the provinces but another eighty-one were still required. A lot of work and a lot of money was at stake – over 75,000 livres.

Unfortunately for Schmidt, the two machines already completed were deemed to be substandard. The Versailles executioner complained: 'On receiving the equipment supplied, the blade from Seine-et-Oise was badly tempered and chipped and there are five people who are due for immediate execution.'

The ingenious inventor, as Dr Louis had referred to him, had been looking forward to retiring on the proceeds from the manufacture of the guillotines, but now his integrity and his future seemed to be under attack from all quarters. Roederer, who was originally quite happy to accept M. Guedon's inflated estimate for the machine, at least until Dr Louis introduced him to Schmidt, was exhibiting signs of paranoia concerning the public purse. It was as if his own pockets were being picked by this greedy little man. Schmidt, however, believed he was the victim of intrigue and treachery as a result of the actions of stingy and untrustworthy officials. There was no neutral ground left to tread, where Schmidt might achieve an amicable settlement to the problem. A head had to roll, even though in this case only metaphorically.

Roederer, cranking up the levels of contention yet again, wrote to the new finance minister on 7 June decrying the avaricious maker of harpsichords:

Due to the inflated price originally quoted by M. Guedon, there was no reason to think that M. Schmidt's machine would do anything other than give him an honest return. Since then I suspect that the machine should cost considerably less than quoted by M. Schmidt. The result of an examination and new estimate of the machine states that it is worth no more than 305 livres or 329 livres if the leather bag is included. The architect has drawn attention to defects in the machine which when rectified will cost an estimated 500 livres for a perfected machine.

Tobias Schmidt rose to the challenge, determined not to be defeated by what he considered to be a bureaucratic conspiracy to rob him of his rightful rewards, including the expenses incurred for the three machines constructed to date. He went as far as to insist that the price of each machine could not be reduced below 824 livres, even on a large order. Behind Roederer's back, he offered his services to supply machines on the black market. After all, the provinces required their own guillotines – and quickly. The number of condemned was growing all the time and to Schmidt business was business.

M. Roederer dug in his heels and on 30 June wrote again to the finance minister, the newly appointed M. Beaulieu, condemning Schmidt's perceived greed. The new blood in the Ministry, determined to demonstrate the utmost efficiency and devotion to the defence of the public purse, agreed wholeheartedly with Roederer's viewpoint. Action was required to bring Schmidt to heel. He was ordered by the minister to explain his activities forthwith and to give reasons in mitigation without further delay.

Unfortunately for Schmidt he was a proud man and his pride encouraged him to believe he was indispensable. After all, he was the man who had constructed the machine and practically owned it; the only difficulty had been the granting of the patent. Somewhat disgruntled, Schmidt foolishly waited more than four weeks before contacting the minister on this urgent matter.

There were further complaints, including some bungled executions. Regardless of the mounting criticism, Schmidt pressed on and by 3 August had prepared a counter-argument in an effort to defend his tarnished reputation. His defence was submitted to M. Le Roulx, yet another new finance minister, the third to date, but one who was no more sympathetic than his predecessors. Schmidt strongly countered the attacks made upon him and his professional ability. Rejecting the complaint of miscarried executions, he blamed the incompetence of the executioner in question. He insisted that a fair price for the manufacture of the guillotine was still 824 livres, and attacked the rapacious Roederer, pointing out his obviously limited knowledge of carpentry. In one last audacious and over-confident display, he requested that the patent he had applied for should be validated without further delay. Such insubordination and abominable cheek, addressed directly to the Ministry, no less, was rewarded accordingly. His patent was denied and his contracts all cancelled. Schmidt lost his guillotine.

The poor man deteriorated quickly. His interest in making musical instruments waned; it could not match the excitement of his other beloved instrument, the guillotine. Like Dr Guillotin, Schmidt survived the Revolution and the Reign of Terror, living into the new era of the Consulate. A confirmed alcoholic, he died while intoxicated and delirious. In his last moments he probably remembered in his dreams, or perhaps nightmares, his contribution to the creation of the greatest passion of his life, the guillotine.

* * *

A new society based on equality had been envisaged for France. But after four traumatic and bloody years of Revolution that Utopian landscape was still a distant dream. The illusion of freedom, particularly freedom of speech, was swept away in the panic and terror. The Jacobin elements of the Revolution were thirsty for blood. Dr Guillotin, a Jacobin himself, had unwittingly proposed the means whereby that thirst could be quenched. The Terror penetrated the very souls of the people, feeding on their hopes, their political aspirations, their fears – and eventually their blood.

The name of Dr Guillotin was abhorred by the visionaries and more feared than the Sansons. The machine named after him had made death upon the high scaffold too easy, too theatrical and too enjoyable for the callous mob's entertainment. Without the guillotine, the Terror could not have gripped France in the all-consuming way that it did. Dr Guillotin himself was close to ruin. He had lost his clients. The very rich had fled to save their lives and others of more moderate means took care to avoid him. Casual acquaintances he met in the street would tap the back of their necks in recognition of what his name represented. For the proud doctor such mockery was insulting and made his already difficult existence intolerable – and now there was danger, immediate and life-threatening. As a Jacobin he had retained his political interests. He remained a member of the 89 Club and in debate had opposed the eloquent but dangerous Maximilien Robespierre, the Deputy from Arras. Cunning and totally ruthless, Robespierre was politically extremely powerful, and known as 'the incorruptible one'. Dr Guillotin should have known better than to confront him. According to one of Robespierre's many informants, Dr Guillotin was quoted as saying of Robespierre, 'He has hell in his face, in his temperament and in his future'. At a later meeting of the Jacobin Club Guillotin's indiscretions provoked an icy stare from Robespierre, which did nothing to increase the doctor's confidence in his own future within the revolutionary arena. The Deputy from Arras and his acolytes were known to be devoid of compassion; clemency was unknown to them. Alarmed, Dr Guillotin realised that it was time for him to hide or die; he took the only sensible action and went into hiding.

On 13 July 1793 the extremist Jean-Paul Marat (a doctor who in pre-revolutionary times was an early advocate of changes in the penal code, particularly as it touched on capital punishment) was assassinated in his bath by the Girondin emissary, Charlotte Corday, a young country girl from Caen. Shortly after Marat's death, a friend warned Dr Guillotin that he was about to be arrested and he fled from Paris. It was now obvious to him that there was no longer room for moderates in politics, or for critics of the powerful Jacobin dynasty. The Jacobins' presence in the National Assembly was overwhelming, their grip on the corridors of power absolute. In haste Guillotin managed to procure a doctor's commission in the French Northern Army, and fled to Arras, the heart of Robespierre's own constituency. Where better to hide? It was certainly the last place anyone would expect to find him.

Safely hidden in Arras, Dr Guillotin carried on with the work that was most dear to him, as a doctor and surgeon aiding mankind. Only when he learned of Robespierre's death on 28 July 1794, ironically in the grip of Dr Guillotin's device, did the good doctor finally return to his home in Paris. Dr Guillotin lived to the age of seventy-seven. His life had been an industrious one and his services to France incalculable. His pioneering work associated with the vaccination procedures devised by the famous Edward Jenner saved many thousands of French lives – many more than ever perished beneath the blade of the guillotine. In 1814, suffering from an anthrax infection, he gently slipped away into a coma and died. He left no heirs, only his wife who outlived him by eighteen years. He would have been distraught that his simple device, created only for the benefit of the people of France, is still known throughout the world by his name.

* * *

The construction of the guillotines for the provinces was proceeding slowly. Although the scaffold in Paris was a permanent structure, the other towns and cities throughout France had no such equipment and it was not unusual for a town which owned a guillotine to lend it to neighbouring towns when the need arose. Such generosity is illustrated by the following letter from the administrator of Avignon:

Dear Friend,
I return the guillotine that the Department of the Gard was kind enough to lend me. It has delivered the Republic from an emigré and three counter-revolutionaries. The Committee has provided the Department of Vaucluse with the guillotine it requires. I thank you for the services rendered.
Vive la République!
Barjavel.

Barjavel's enthusiasm soon waned when he realised that, although Avignon now had its very own guillotine, the district had no executioner! He had to borrow one from his friend from the Gard, who by good fortune employed two in his own jurisdiction. Unusually, the scaffold in Avignon became a permanent fixture, located in the Place de l'Horloge.

The delay experienced in producing the guillotine en masse was itself a bonus. If there was no guillotine available for use, then no one could be guillotined! However, after the Revolution the device spread beyond the boundaries of France into every corner of the French Empire. Wherever Napoleon conquered and French imperialism spread, there was the guillotine. In the nineteenth century the guillotine was used in Italy; the literary genius Charles Dickens attended an execution in Rome in 1845, five decades after the machine's invention. He was not impressed by what he saw and found the whole ritual sickening and distasteful. The guillotine was later to feature in his novel of the French Revolution, *A Tale of Two Cities*, in which the hero Sydney Carton redeems his dissolute behaviour by going to the scaffold in order to safeguard the happiness of those who have become most precious to him.

The execution Dickens witnessed was of a man condemned to death for the murder of a Bavarian countess. It was supposed to take place at 8.45am but in fact it did not take place until much later in the day. The scaffold had been erected, appropriately enough, near the church of San Giovanni Decollato (St John the Baptist was beheaded by Herod Antipas to please Salome). Dickens described the execution:

[The scaffold was] an untidy, unpainted, uncouth, crazy-looking thing some seven feet high with a tall gallows-shaped frame rising above it in which was the knife, charged with a ponderous weight of iron all ready to descend and glittering brightly in the morning sun . . . monks were seen approaching the scaffold from the church carrying the effigy of Christ upon the cross . . . this was carried around the foot of the scaffold and placed at the front so that the criminal might see it to the last . . . he appeared on the platform barefooted, his hands bound and with the collar and neck of his shirt cut away almost to the shoulder. A young man of

A Simple Device

six and twenty vigorously made and well shaped . . . he immediately kneeled down beneath the knife, his neck fitting into a hole made for the purpose . . . exactly like a pillory. Immediately below him was a leathern bag and into it his head rolled instantly . . . the knife had fallen heavily and with a rattling sound . . . A strange appearance was the apparent annihilation of the neck. The head was taken off so close that it seemed as if the knife had narrowly escaped crushing the jaw . . . The body looked as if there was nothing left above the shoulder . . . It was an ugly careless sickening spectacle meaning nothing but butchery.

Charles Dickens was appalled by the guillotine, but this was not a sentiment universally shared. In 1817 Lord Byron wrote to his friend John Murray, full of enthusiasm for the splendid instrument of death:

The day before I left Rome I saw three robbers guillotined – the ceremony – including the *masqued* priests – the half-naked executioners – the bandaged criminals – the black Christ & his banner – the scaffold – the soldiery – the slow procession – & the quick rattle and heavy fall of the axe – the splash of the blood – & the ghastliness of the exposed heads – is altogether more impressive than the vulgar and ungentlemanly dirty 'new drop' & dog-like agony of infliction upon the sufferers of the English sentence [i.e. hanging]. The head was taken off before the eye could trace the blow – but from an attempt to draw back the head – notwithstanding it was held forward by the hair – the first head was cut off close to the ears – the other two were taken off more cleanly; – it is better than the Oriental way [i.e. with sword] – & (I should think) than the axe of our ancestors. The pain seems little – & yet the effect to the spectator – & the preparation to the criminal – is very striking & chilling. The first turned me quite hot & thirsty – & made me shake so that I could hardly hold the opera-glass (I was close – but determined to see – as one should see everything once – with attention) the second and third (which shows how dreadfully soon things grow indifferent) I am ashamed to say had no effect on me – as a horror – though I would have saved them if I could.

Dickens's observations were written almost thirty years after Byron's. Perhaps the difference of opinion reflected the period in which each man lived. Byron was essentially a man of the eighteenth century, his beliefs and experiences of life and death exemplifying the period of the French Revolution and Napoleonic expansion. Charles Dickens was a man of the nineteenth century and his works made his readers vividly aware of the brutality and harshness of life; he demanded change and a more humanitarian outlook.

* * *

On 21 January 1793 the guillotine was assembled upon its high scaffold in the Place de la Révolution, between the remains of the statue of Louis XV and the entrance to the Champs-Elysées. On this terrible day the guillotine was to claim the life of its most august victim, Louis XVI himself. Standing close by the machine was the executioner of the city of Paris, an hereditary office-holder in his own right. From the mid-seventeenth century a Sanson had been the 'maître des basses et hautes oeuvres', a post ratified by the king. On this cold and bleak winter morning it was ironic that the 'king's executioner' should indeed be the executioner of the king.

The king's death was the inevitable conclusion of the political struggles between the two main factions of the National Convention – the Girondins (or 'Plains') and the Jacobins (or 'Mountain'). Their nicknames were derived from the seating arrangements for the separate parties within the hall of the Convention. The Girondins, although accepting the king's supposed guilt, had no real desire for his death. It was an awkward situation for them. The death of the king might well alienate the more moderate factions of the recently elected but as yet uncommitted representatives of the Convention. But if they publicly voted for the king's reprieve, they would inevitably be accused of having betrayed their political principles, and such an act of open defiance might encourage Robespierre to accuse them of having royalist sympathies and to accuse them of treason. The king's death would cause the reactionary forces at work in the Assembly to splinter, allowing the nation to freewheel into the Reign of Terror. The king himself was merely a piece on the revolutionary chessboard, a pawn to be sacrificed for political reasons, and after his death a new and fiercer game would begin. The issue of the king's execution could not be avoided diplomatically and Jacobin influence and pressure ensured Girondin complicity. The same influence and pressure would be later used again to bring about the downfall and execution of all the main members of the Girondins. The mountain would indeed come crashing down upon the plains.

The appearance of the king upon the scaffold was the prelude to a whole series of executions, which seemed to be infinite during the Reign of Terror. It was now possible for those in power to destroy their enemies much more quickly than ever before – a powerful reminder of the guillotine's frightful potential. Upon the terrible day of the king's death, which even Sanson had been dreading, the significance of the guillotine would take on an entirely new dimension. At its outset the Revolution had striven to achieve the dream of natural goodness and fairness to all. But such intellectual concepts had a powerful emotional counterpart – the heart versus the head. Since the guillotine was a machine for slicing off heads, it symbolised the revolutionary belief in the qualities of the heart. The execution of the king would not only remove from office the head of state, but also destroy the father figure at the heart of the nation, once deemed to be sacred. The presence of the guillotine would have a deeper underlying significance from that point on. Though still feared, the guillotine would become respected and almost sanctified.

* * *

Louis XVI was not an unpopular monarch initially, but he forfeited the hearts of his subjects and lost his life at the age of thirty-nine beneath the blade of the guillotine. Louis was only twenty years of age when he was crowned king of France. He took as his queen an Austrian princess named Antoinette, known afterwards as Marie-Antoinette. It was the first time that a French monarch had taken an Austrian wife and their marriage would bring the princess to a country where enmity towards Austria had endured for centuries. By the standards of the time the good-natured Louis was a virtuous king, but his nation was governed in a feudal manner. His queen, though never really trusted or loved by the people, was young and beautiful, two attributes that served to provide her with a measure of respect. The country and its finances had not kept pace with changes in the wider world and were in desperate need of reform. The French people, anxious and agitated, nevertheless maintained their deference to the monarchy and held fast to the belief that their new sovereign might prove to be the nation's salvation. Louis was acutely aware that his country required political and financial reform, but he was at a loss as to how he could achieve such reforms.

During the Revolution it became clear that in the struggle for equality the people would no longer tolerate unwarranted privileges for society's elite. As their agitation increased, the people looked to their monarch for strong and decisive leadership that would release them from the misery and pains of life. The king understood the situation but seemed unable to combat the growing resentment. He soon began to appear to the people as weak and indecisive, a flawed character whose autocratic powers were directed against his subjects. Even at this late stage, if Louis had been able to muster a degree of common sense he might still have survived the coming storm and perhaps maintained the monarchy within the new democracy. But despite the best of intentions he plunged into one error of judgement after another, exacerbating the situation still further.

Louis had been perplexed by the American War of

Independence some thirteen years previously. Reluctant to offend his English neighbours, he had fought to maintain French neutrality in the conflict but was unable to prevent Lafayette taking ship to America to aid General Washington. His weakness damaged his fragile relationship with England. At a time when Louis urgently needed to reinforce his links with his neighbours he was unable to do so, and the French monarchy became isolated.

The king's Comptroller-General of Finance, Anne Robert Jacques Turgot, a man of vision, understood the nature of the rising tide of uneasiness that had started to engulf France and put forward his ideas on reforming the taxation laws. His proposals favoured the people and it would have stood the king in good stead if he had backed the reforms. However, under pressure from the nobility to reject the proposals outright, Louis dithered and refused to support Turgot. As ever, he was caught between the two opposing factions and lacked the strength to take control of the situation.

The wealthy financier Jacques Necker also tried to prop up the ailing economy with grandiose schemes involving enormous sums of money; he also proposed the borrowing of substantial reserves from other countries in order to give the French economy a temporary respite and improve the financial state of the people. But once again, the entrenched and avaricious nobility pressured Louis into rejecting Necker's ideas.

In an effort to stem the rising tide of discontent the king called upon the States General to convene in 1789 – the first time this had happened in 175 years. The body of the state comprised three factions: the nobility, the clergy and the people. The subjects of France still retained their loyalty to the king, and the people's representatives present at the meeting still looked to their sovereign to provide the leadership that would bring about an improved way of life for one and all. At the heart of the problem lay the delicate question of power-sharing, but Louis failed to see the dangers that lay ahead. At this critical time in the history of France, it was privilege that was on trial, and not the king.

The principal dilemma facing the king was whether to ratify the new scheme whereby the States General (effectively the French Parliament) would be entitled to vote on national issues as one body, which was the desire of the people's representatives. The alternative, strongly supported by the nobility and the clergy, was for the three factions to remain separate and to vote accordingly as independent bodies. This, of course, would leave power firmly in the hands of the nobility, supported by the clergy. Louis did not act quickly enough and lost the initiative; when he tried to reach a compromise, the beleaguered and now impatient people's representatives declared that they would create a new National Assembly and take charge of taxation. Louis, under intense pressure from the nobility, was poorly advised and rashly ordered the new National Assembly to close. The delegates, now furious and their patience at an end, invaded the indoor tennis courts at the palace of Versailles and swore an oath to uphold the rights of man. Known as the Tennis Court Oath, this declaration signalled the first stirrings of the coming Revolution. If only Louis had supported the Assembly, how different his future might have been.

On 14 July 1789 hungry Parisians, whipped into a frenzy by extremists and agitators, stormed the prison fortress of the Bastille, that hated symbol of the king's authority. In provincial France châteaux were also attacked and looted. The king still did nothing but waited cautiously in the Palace of Versailles. Far-sighted advisers who could see the rising storm urged him to support the new Constitution, but the nobility and the clergy urged him to crush it by force. Louis now made his fatal error of judgement. He did nothing.

On 5 October the starving mob marched to the Palace of Versailles demanding bread. Following a night of lawlessness and mayhem, the king and queen, together with their numerous retainers, became the 'guests' of the people. They were taken back to Paris and lodged in the Tuileries, effectively prisoners as their world fell about them. They would never see Versailles again. In the midst of the turbulence, the Assembly convened and began to focus its attention on the revision of the antiquated penal code, a movement spearheaded by Dr Guillotin.

Opinions in the National Assembly remained divided on what action should be taken over the royal family, now under guard in the Tuileries. All but a very small minority still considered the retention of the monarchy a viable proposition, albeit in some new and revised form. Marie-Antoinette hoped that her brother Leopold of Austria would seize the opportunity to invade France while the country remained in political turmoil. The Austrian and Prussian alliance would then be able to reinstate the French monarchy and quash the Revolution in its infancy. It was not to happen.

The Comte de Mirabeau, one of Louis's wisest advisers, offered a compromise: a constitutional monarchy similar to that in England, but this plan came to nought as he was distrusted by the extremists in the Assembly and by the queen. She was still urging her husband to adopt a plan for invasion and rescue. Mirabeau was subsequently elected president of the Assembly, in January 1791, but soon afterwards died, leaving the unfortunate Louis virtually devoid of any counsel save that of the queen. In June of that year Count Axel Fersen of Sweden, a supporter of the queen, organised a daring escape plan. The royal family would be taken from the Tuileries to Verdun, where they would be met by an escort who would take them out of France. The plan failed when the coach stopped at Varennes and the king was recognised. The royal family was taken back to the Tuileries, this time under house arrest. The king was no longer trusted. When his apartments within the Tuileries were searched, incriminating evidence was discovered. The king was given no choice but to accept the new Constitution. He was also forced to declare war on Austria and Prussia. Both these nations had openly defied the new France, stating that should the monarchy there not be restored, the French would have to bear the inevitable consequences. Initially the war went badly for France. The king and queen were both accused of treachery, of fraternising with the enemies of the nation. On 10 August 1792 a frenzied mob attacked the Tuileries, slaughtering the Swiss Guard entrusted with the king and queen's safety. The royal family fled to the Riding School, where the Convention was meeting in a state of nervous agitation. For three days the family was kept hostage, taking refuge in a small reporters' room. They were finally removed to the Temple prison and held there under armed guard. For Louis and Marie-Antoinette it was the beginning of the end; they were doomed and there was no chance of rescue.

In Paris the violence continued. On 2 September the prisons were attacked by the mob and those held there massacred. A nervous public had no wish to volunteer for the war effort and leave their families unprotected when the prisons were overflowing with the enemies of France. On 20 September the revolutionary Army commanded by General Dumouriez won the battle of Valmy, defeating the Prussians. This left the king and queen completely isolated and any lingering hopes they may have entertained of a possible escape simply faded away.

The death of the king had now become a necessity. His trial lasted three days, the outcome being decided by 721 men: 387 voted for death and 334 for life. Whatever else Louis was, he was not a coward. He may not have been a good king, but he would die like one, without remorse or recriminations. God and courage would be his salvation and forgiveness his code. On 21 January 1793 the king went to his death upon the guillotine.

The morning was misty and bitterly cold. For the first time the guillotine had been erected at the Place de la Révolution. The Convention, apprehensive that a last-minute rescue might be attempted, decided that the route to the Place de la Révolution along the wide and spacious rue Royale would be easier to police than the narrow, congested streets leading to the Place du Carrousel, the guillotine's previous location. The carriage conveying the king was heavily guarded by 12,000 well-armed men and more than 50,000 members of the Garde Nationale formed a line from the Temple to the execution square (now called the Place de la Concorde). On his final journey the king was accompanied by the Abbé Edgeworth de

Firmont, an Irish priest. The carriage slowly emerged out of the silent, heavily armed multitude into the large empty area that had been left at the foot of the scaffold. The presence of the multitude gave the impression that the whole of Paris had turned out to watch their king die. When the coach stopped, the king whispered to the abbé, 'We have arrived, if I am not mistaken.' An assistant executioner stepped forward and opened the door of the coach. Louis turned to the gendarmes and addressed them thus: 'Messieurs, I commend this gentleman to your care; be good enough to see that after my death he is not offered any insult. I charge you to ensure this!' The king then dismounted from the coach.

The events of that fateful day were reported in the newspaper *Thermomètre du Jour*, but the facts were somewhat misrepresented. Stepping out of character, Sanson the executioner felt compelled to write to the newspaper and explain exactly what transpired. Abbé Edgeworth, who remained with the king until the end, also recorded the scene.

As soon as the king stepped down from the carriage, three assistant executioners approached him in order to remove his outer garments. The king, still retaining the dignity of a monarch, pushed them away and removed his coat himself. He also took off his collar and made himself ready. The assistants came forward again, this time to bind his hands. The king indignantly refused to allow his hands to be tied. The executioners informed him that it was absolutely necessary to bind him before the execution could proceed. Louis looked to his confessor, as though for counsel. The Abbé, in tears, said to the king, 'Sire, in accepting this outrage, I see one final resemblance between Your Majesty and the Saviour Who is about to be your reward.' With an expression of sadness the king raised his eyes towards heaven and replied, 'Surely it needs nothing less than His example to make me submit to such an insult.' Holding his hands out to be bound he said, 'Do what you must, I shall drink the cup even to the dregs.'

The king asked Sanson if the drums would go on beating all the time, but was informed that the executioner did not know.

Louis mounted the steep steps of the scaffold and on the platform tried to press forward to the front as though he wished to speak, but he was again told that this was impossible. The king was led to the guillotine and was strapped to the *bascule*. At this moment he cried out, 'People, I die innocent!' Turning to the executioners he said, 'Messieurs, I am innocent of all I am accused of. I hope that my blood may cement the happiness of the French people.' Those were the last words of the king of France.

* * *

The popular journalist Louis-Sébastien Mercier, who had earned a reputation as a prophet of doom and frequently foretold the king's death, seems to have been cast down by the popular reaction to the king's execution, and wrote a piece registering his disgust at the festivities that the execution unleashed:

> His blood flowed and cries of joy from eighty thousand armed men struck my ears. . . . I saw the schoolboys of the Quatre-Nations throw their hats in the air; his blood flowed and some dipped their fingers in it, or a pen or a piece of paper; one tasted it and it was well salted. An executioner on the boards of the scaffold sold and distributed little packets of hair and the ribbon that bound them; each piece carried a little fragment of his clothes or some bloody vestige of that tragic scene. I saw people pass by, arm in arm, laughing, chatting familiarly, as if they were at a fête.

Louis endured his end with a fortitude that impressed even the executioners. Sanson was convinced that the king's qualities emanated from his religious principles.

The guillotine was not discriminating: it had taken the head of a king and it would do likewise to a queen. Sanson was painfully aware that it could also beckon to an executioner who showed too much compassion for his victims. The letter he wrote to the newspaper *Thermomètre du Jour* had contained an unmistakable thread of sympathy and even admiration for the late king. Such opinions were easily misconstrued, and could be very dangerous not only for the writer but also for his publisher. To stand up for one's principles was one thing, but to go to the guillotine for them was quite another matter. M. Dulaure, reporter for the newspaper, thought it wise to add certain observations to Sanson's candid letter, lest he be accused of endorsing the contents. He wrote:

> How is it possible to combine religious principles which condemn crimes of perfidy and treason with the demonstrated crimes and perfidies of Louis? How could the consciousness of his own crimes be allied with the fortitude of innocence? Louis was either more obstinate in his criminal opinions than most men or his hypocrisy accompanied him to his death; or else he was the most fanatical, the most credulous, and the most imbecile of all those whom the Priests have blinded.

In revolutionary France, in the shadow of the guillotine, discretion was always the better part of valour, whether for journalists or executioners. Sanson had executed a condemned man now referred to simply as Louis Capet, but in his mind he still saw a royal figure. After the execution of the king, Sanson knew for certain that Marie-Antoinette was doomed to face the same fate.

An interesting question has arisen concerning the royal executions. Did Charles-Henri Sanson actually execute the king or was it another man? The official documentation clearly states that Charles-Henri Sanson was the officially appointed executioner, both at the time of the king's death and later during the Reign of Terror. Born in 1739, he held the office as a hereditary prerogative, just as his father had done before him. He was fifty-four years old at the time of the execution and had been in active service for some forty years. However, in Abbé Edgeworth de Firmont's account of the king's execution he states that he distinctly saw the youngest of the executioners operating the guillotine. This cannot have been Sanson.

Months later, when that most tragic of victims, Marie-Antoinette, was executed in October 1793, a turnkey named Laravière left an account of the queen's last hours of confinement in her bleak prison cell. He mentions that it was Henri Sanson, then a young man, who had prepared the queen for her execution.

One year later, in 1794, the Abbé Carrichon produced an account of a series of executions that took place during the Terror in which he stated that the executioner was a 'young' man. All of these authentic eye-witness narratives contradict the assumption that Charles-Henri Sanson carried out the executions. Perhaps the explanation lies in Sanson himself. When he first saw the guillotine in action, Sanson had declared it to be a fine machine, as long as its facility was not abused. Perhaps he felt that it had been abused, to such an extent that he felt only repugnance. Perhaps this encouraged him to leave the executions to his proficient son Henri, who may have been less sensitive about the misuse of the guillotine and therefore carried out the executions on his father's behalf.

Did Henri Sanson kill the king? It seems likely, for how else could his father so distinctly remember all the little details concerning the execution if he had been busy with the actual deed – and certainly Charles-Henri Sanson had no desire to take the life of his monarch in an act of regicide, state-sponsored or not.

* * *

Upon the scaffold the king's head was displayed to the shouting, jeering mob. His death had been the wish of the new rulers of France. The king's own cousin, Philippe Egalité, formerly the Duc d'Orléans, had voted for his death. Told of this just before his execution, Louis exclaimed sadly, 'How can such a man as this exist?' The greater tragedy for Louis was that so many men of his cousin's ilk held sway in the Assembly.

Worse, their lust for royal blood was not yet satisfied. It was as though the revolutionary government believed that the royal blood would wash away its fears, but in fact it did no more than compound and intensify them. Louis's death was meant to offer absolution to the ruling powers, but it was not enough. Distrust and contention continued to tear apart the various factions of the Assembly.

With his last words the king denied his guilt and spoke of his wish for harmony among the people of his nation. He died not as a tyrant but as a man who defended freedom of speech to the end. The paranoid powers that had condemned him, however, had become so disorientated that they were not satisfied just to control the lives of the people – they wanted to be able to influence what the nation should be allowed to believe in. The right to individuality was in jeopardy. The decision to execute the king was a mistake; his death made him a martyr and through his death he achieved a kind of victory.

It was Louis the king who had gone bravely to the scaffold, setting a fine example to all who would follow, but it was Louis the man whose calm nature and forbearance had been a source of strength to his wife. They had faced many dangers together, caught up in the fervour of the Revolution, but now he was gone. The tragic and unhappy queen stood alone, without friends or spiritual comfort and surrounded by those whose only desire was for her death.

No one will know how Marie-Antoinette maintained her sanity during this period, but somehow she did. She doubtless took comfort from her faith and her trust in God just as her husband had before his death. Through the trauma of her own farcical trial she remained composed and calm. Her trial had been no more than an evil and slanderous attack upon her character, and the outcome was inevitable. She knew the Tribunal wanted her death and that there would be no appeal. Aware of her impending condemnation, she bore it all with indefatigable dignity.

In the final months of her life the queen had learned of the death of the Jacobin extremist Marat and of the rebellions in the provinces. She was aware of the imminent invasion of France by its enemies. Just a week after her husband's death the National Assembly had declared war on the old enemy, England. She knew that the new Jacobin supremacy needed not just to take action but to be seen taking it if France were to be saved from the turmoil. The former queen was a symbol of the powers that threatened to bring down the Revolution, just as the guillotine symbolised all that could save it. The queen and the guillotine were inexorably linked together.

By 1 August the queen, referred to now as the Widow Capet, was removed from the Temple to a small cell within the Conciergerie prison, the antechamber of the guillotine. This was to be her home for the next two months and all the time she knew her fate was sealed. To further embarrass the queen, her cell door had been altered and lowered in height so that whenever she was visited by the Convention's representatives she was compelled to bow before them on leaving her cell.

Following her shameful trial the Tribunal deliberated for just an hour before sentencing her to death. Marie-Antoinette made no response to the verdict but merely shook her head in disdain. She was innocent and she remained calm. In less than twelve months this Austrian princess and queen of France had been deprived of her throne and of her liberty. She had been widowed by the executioner and now she was separated from her children. Alone and without hope she faced the guillotine herself.

Charles-Henri Sanson, who had been ordered to execute the king just ten months previously, was instructed to guillotine the queen of France. He requested that a closed carriage be obtained to convey the queen to the scaffold. Members of the Public Safety Committee were consulted but had no opinion on the matter either way and left the decision to the Principal Prosecutor of the Tribunal, Fouquier Tinville. To his everlasting disgrace, he decided that in order to further denigrate and humiliate the queen she should be conveyed to her death in a common cart.

Sanson and his son Henri, who may have been the

executioner in lieu of his father, entered the Conciergerie at 10am on 16 October 1793. An usher of the Tribunal accompanied the executioners to where the queen was waiting. Marie-Antoinette rose from her seat and walked courageously towards them. Rather weakly she addressed them: 'I am ready, gentlemen, we can set out.' How sad a figure she was now to those who knew her in her former glory. The tragedies she had suffered had taken a terrible toll on her appearance. Even her fine hair had thinned and turned white, and yet she appeared calm and unemotional. She wore a plain white piqué dress and her hair, tied with a black ribbon, was covered by a small bonnet. Covering her shoulders was a white muslin fichu. Henri Sanson, on behalf of his father, prepared the queen for the guillotine and led her out to the Cour de Mai where a tumbrel awaited her.

No doubt the queen had assumed that, like the king, she would be granted the courtesy of a closed carriage. Fouquier Tinville's mindless cruelty would subject her to the vicious mob that lined the streets, howling abuse at her. As she stepped out into the Cour de Mai and caught sight of the tumbrel, which was little better than a dung-cart, she momentarily lost her composure. She asked Sanson to untie her hands and in the corner of the courtyard, without even a semblance of privacy, she relieved herself. Her hands were again tied behind her back and she took her seat in the tumbrel, facing to the rear. It was a tradition of the executioner that the victims of the guillotine should not see the terrifying implement until the last moment had come. Marie-Antoinette's journey through the streets of Paris, now lined by soldiers and the inevitable screaming mob, lasted almost an hour. The jeering rabble behaved predictably and showed not the slightest degree of compassion for this sad, solitary figure. A woman in the crowd spat saliva into her hand and with a scream of defiance threw it towards the queen, who calmly turned away. She hardly looked at the jeering, hooting mob, maintaining her composure with a show of indifference.

While in prison Marie-Antoinette had declined the services of the Abbé Lothringer, who had forsaken his own principles and sworn an oath of fidelity to the Republic. His repeated requests to be allowed to accompany her to the scaffold had annoyed her but she finally yielded and allowed him to set out with her on the final journey. Perhaps he saw in the queen that courage and inner strength that he had lost. There was one bright moment in that dismal journey. It is recorded that a priest whom the queen greatly respected had managed to communicate with her and promised to give her absolution on her journey to the guillotine. In the rue St-Honoré she noticed a particular house and, at a given sign that she alone understood, recognised the priest. She lowered her head, prayed for the forgiveness of God and for her salvation; an enigmatic smile came to her lips and was reflected in her eyes. She was no longer alone.

The scaffold for her execution had been erected in the Place de la Révolution between the Pedestal and the garden of the Tuileries. The tumbrel came slowly to a halt and she moved wearily forward to clamber down from the cart. Henri Sanson quickly came forward and took her hand in his as if to guide her steps, and whispered 'Have courage, Madame.' The queen responded in a whisper, saying 'Thank you, sir, thank you.'

Declining further assistance, the queen approached the steps of the scaffold, but slightly stumbled and trod upon Sanson's foot. She immediately apologised, saying, 'I beg your pardon, Monsieur, I did not mean to do that.' Then she climbed the steep steps of the scaffold to face her death. She looked for the last time towards the beautiful gardens of the Tuileries with its memories of happier times. Then the *bascule* was tipped down and propelled towards the uprights of the guillotine. In a second, Marie-Antoinette was no more.

5

Terror

The appearance of the guillotine was ill timed. As the revolutionary impetus accelerated out of control and rushed headlong towards panic, mayhem and the Terror, the ideals and moral codes of the high-minded men behind the drive for a republic foundered and perished. The next eighteen months represented one of France's worst periods, racked with judicial murder and chaos. Standing tall in the midst of the confusion and political intrigue was the guillotine, a constant factor amid the chaos. The machine was mounted permanently in the Place de la Révolution and the whole of Paris became its antechamber. Almost as feared as the guillotine was the massive and forbidding Conciergerie, the Parisian prison. With its lofty dark towers and curtain walls, it was an impregnable fortress, a medieval keep that housed the potential victims of the guillotine.

Citizens on the quai de la Mégisserie could look to the opposite bank and see the Palais de Justice, which stood between two bridges across the Seine, the Pont-Neuf and the Pont au Change. Further along were three large towers, part of the Conciergerie, on the quai de l'Horloge. On the east side of the Palais the courtyard of the prison gave access to the busy streets, with houses and shops of all dimensions filling up every available space. The gateway to the prison courtyard was situated on the boulevard du Palais. The whole area echoed to the melancholy sound of a large bell, its reverberations bouncing gloomily off the surrounding buildings and walls. It was the saddest of sounds, for

79

everyone knew that it heralded the dreaded arrival of Sanson's tumbrels at the prison to collect the day's victims for their last journey to the guillotine.

Two large bays within the prison were occupied by the guards and men-at-arms, the larger bay being known as the Salle des Gens d'Armes. Between the Salle des Gardes and the rue de Paris were kept the poor prisoners and vagrants, those individuals without money or other resources. They slept at night on the hard, cold, stone floor and the area was so crowded that prison guards would often stand on people while looking for some particular individual. The atmosphere was heavy and fetid. At night flaming torch light briefly illuminated the darkness, casting long shadows. The lives of the prisoners seemed part of a human tontine, but there would be no winner. Each day, time was the only prize awarded – another twenty-four hours of life.

At daylight the prisoner's gallery adjacent to the rue de Paris was noisy and bustling. Interest centred on the numerous lawyers, arriving, conferring with clients or the Tribunal and then departing. In addition there were many policemen and jailers, all busy checking names, compiling lists and verifying identifications amid the vast number of prisoners herded together like cattle waiting for slaughter.

* * *

From the first floor comes a prisoner, escorted by guards down a spiral staircase from the Tour Bonbec or Bonbec Tower, originally a torture chamber. Its crenellated structure once confined François Damiens, the victim of unspeakable cruelty and torture. The prisoner is marched along a gallery and into the Parloir, an anteroom to the men's prison yard. On the far wall of the Parloir is a staircase leading to a room within which the prisoner will come face to face with the revolutionary Tribunal, callous men, impersonal and seemingly incapable of clemency. For now they reign supreme, new masters not of freedom but of the choking enslavement of liberalism.

Terror

Fouquier Tinville, the much-feared Public Prosecutor, works at night by candlelight in his small office within the Tour César compiling lists for the next day's drama, condemning to death as many as sixty men and women each day. To him they are faceless victims of no importance to the Revolution. For Fouquier Tinville it is the numbers that are important. The guillotine waiting in the Place de la Révolution has become the extremist's god, demanding human sacrifice on an unthinkable scale.

The prisoner waits within the Parloir, knowing all too well that his life is forfeit. Later in the day, after passing through the hands of the Tribunal, he is taken to a holding room and from there to a neighbouring room. Along with all the others he sits on a long timber bench to receive the *toilette du condamné*. The hair is cropped short and the shirt collar removed: nothing must be allowed to obstruct the fall of the blade. With eleven others the prisoner is then led through the women's courtyard and beyond to a corner of the yard known as the 'place of twelve'. For only two minutes they wait here, saying their farewells to the people they recognise. Some ask the inevitable question 'Why me?' – but it is too late for understanding. It is courage they need now. At the sound of the tumbrel bell, the twelve hopeless souls are led to a wicket gate where a clerk of the Tribunal checks their names and ushers them into the Cour de Mai and the waiting tumbrels. As the carts jolt forward out of the courtyard the condemned notice the tricoteuses, those sinister women who sit upon the steps in the courtyard endlessly knitting, watching with grim intensity as the carts pass by with the day's sacrifice for the guillotine.

* * *

Within the Conciergerie the authorities took no notice of the sound of the tumbrel bell announcing the arrival of Sanson's carts. They were always too busy, their workload never ceasing. In the twisting stairways and dark shadows of this bleak building, where cruelty, misery and revulsion prevailed, madness took a firm hold, defying sanity and reason for the next eighteen months. The anonymous twilight world of the Conciergerie was at the very heart of the Terror. As many as 1,200 prisoners were incarcerated at any one time within the fortress walls, and the untiring efforts of the revolutionary Tribunal ensured that 90 per cent of the individuals brought to trial were sent to the guillotine.

Among the poor souls locked within its walls were Marie-Antoinette, the queen of France; the king's sister Madame Elisabeth; Madame du Barry, Louis XV's favourite (she had to be dragged, screaming for her life, to the guillotine – a spectacle which for the first time inspired the sympathy of the crowds witnessing the executions); Charlotte Corday, who assassinated the Jacobin extremist Marat; Madame Roland, the wife of the Minister of the Interior Jean-Marie Roland, who wrote her memoirs while awaiting execution; Philippe Egalité, a cousin of Louis XVI and formerly the Duc d'Orléans; the poet André Chénier; the chemist Lavoisier, who discovered oxygen; countless Girondins, who were all denounced by Danton; Georges Danton himself and fifteen of his supporters, including Camille Desmoulins, denounced by Robespierre; Maximilien Robespierre and twenty of his followers including St-Just, arrested and condemned by the moderates of the Thermidor Convention battling for their own survival; and Fouquier Tinville and the Tribunal judges, reaping the harvest that they had sown.

Desmoulins left a remarkable testimony to the emotional power of the guillotine, a letter written to his beloved wife Lucille as he waited to die:

Camille Desmoulins to his wife on the eve of his execution, 1794:
My Lucile, *ma poule*, despite my torment I believe there is a God, my blood will efface my faults, I will see you again one day O my Lucile . . . is the death which will deliver me from the spectacle of so many crimes such a misfortune? Adieu Loulou, adieu my life, my soul, my divinity on earth . . . I feel

the river banks of life receding before me, I see you again Lucile, I see my arms locked about you, my tied hands embracing you, my severed head resting on you. I am going to die . . .

Almost all these people went to their death with dignity, showing tremendous composure in the face of the large, often vociferous crowd. Danton tried to embrace his colleague de Séchelles in a display of revolutionary solidarity but they were abruptly separated by Sanson – at which Danton is reported to have said: 'They will not prevent our heads from meeting in the basket.' Danton's last words to Sanson were 'Don't forget to show my head to the people. It is well worth the trouble.'

During the eighteen months of the Terror more than 2,500 people passed through the Conciergerie prison on their way to the guillotine. Though the guillotine was swift, the road to the scaffold was tortuously slow, one last ordeal before the victims of the dread machine reached the Place de la Révolution. Two invisible companions, fortitude and faith, rode alongside them in the tumbrels, strengthening the hearts of the day's victims. Faith protected their souls and drove away the horrors of the theatre of hell that they had now entered, for did not Jesus Christ himself speak of their salvation: 'I am the resurrection and the life'? Louis XVI had shown the people how an honourable man should die, and his example was followed time and time again.

* * *

There are three carts today. Sanson the executioner rides in the first cart next to the driver. Each cart holds twelve condemned, now embarked on the road to their own Calvary, their cross the scarlet Timbers of Justice. Trundling out through the gates of the Palais de Justice, the tumbrels turn left into the rue St Barthélémi, heading back towards the Conciergerie, and then left again at the great clock tower, the Tour de l'Horloge. A multitude of onlookers stretches all the way back to the riverbank, howling and shouting obscenities at their former masters in anticipation of their fate.

On this day Sanson has chosen a different route to the scaffold. Instead of travelling down the quayside beneath the towers of the prison, the tumbrels cross the Pont au Change into the cooler and fresher air on the other side of the river, escaping the fetid atmosphere emanating from the large crowd. But not for long. The mob on the quai de la Mégisserie is substantial and for a moment almost stops the slow procession of the carts. In the far distance Sanson can see the trees lining the bank of the Seine in the gardens of the Tuileries, and just beyond, but not yet visible, is his ultimate destination.

As the tumbrels turn back towards the Pont-Neuf the condemned catch their last sight of the Conciergerie. Some may also notice the house of Madame Roland in the Place Dauphine. The wife of a Girondin politician, Madame Roland would herself make that same journey to the scaffold and at the minute of her death cry out 'Oh Liberty! What crimes are committed in thy name!'

The tumbrels continue to jolt through the narrow streets of the rue de la Monnaie and rue du Roule; the crowds are much smaller here. Along the rue Chausetterie the procession slows and at last enters the rue St-Honoré, heading east on the long road to the guillotine. Though the crowds are smaller here, faces stare out of every window in every building they pass. Some shout out obscenities, some wave and others remain silent as though in sympathy. The carts groan and creak as they slowly make their way past the Palais-Royal and its once-beautiful gardens. Passing the street that contains the Jacobin Club there suddenly descends a silence, for there is no mob present. Loitering here has been prohibited. Not far away, in the Maison Duplay, lives the leader of the revolutionary extremists, Maximilien Robespierre. As usual the shutters of his windows are closed.

The journey has taken over an hour. At the end of the rue St-Honoré the horse pulling the first cart is suddenly halted to allow the others to catch up. Sanson watches the approaching carts over his shoulder but carefully avoids looking at the forlorn faces of his passengers. Then the carts move off again together, turning into the rue Royale. Those standing in the tumbrels can now hear the large crowd roaring in anticipation and they turn around nervously. They see the once-picturesque square of Louis XV, now the Place de la Révolution, where a statue of freedom looks down upon the masses. The shouts of the crowds recede as they catch their first glimpse of the guillotine on its lofty scaffold, its two long arms stretching upwards to the clear blue sky.

* * *

The guillotine was seen by the Establishment as a formidable weapon during the uncertain times of the Revolution. For the extremists it proved to be the most powerful tool available to them for purging society of their enemies, whether real or imagined. No organisation or individual was safe from its unremitting censure. The atheist government's disposition had also turned against the Church, whose influence was regarded as a hindrance to the revolutionary dream of a free society. Religion was seen as a burden that had already incapacitated the populace. For those who refused to cooperate with the new order, the sentence was death. The guillotine was neither selective nor discriminating; it was all-embracing, the personification of destruction and a vital tool for the revolutionary extremists. Paradoxically, France remained a Christian country, even though the number of active Christians was dwindling daily. The guillotine had now become the new subject of adoration and worship.

The guillotine was eminently practical, but it had its disadvantages too. The major problem in the use of the guillotine was the blood. At multiple executions, which became the hallmark of the Tribunal's efforts to rid itself of its enemies, there would be gallons of it. Decapitation was instantaneous but for a few moments the heart continued to pump blood through the arteries – blood that spurted out over the base of the apparatus, saturating the floor of the scaffold and the street below. Ironically, the copious amounts of blood were considered to be a greater hazard to public health than the machine itself. At night dogs would congregate in packs to lap up the pools of blood that had accumulated at the base of the scaffold.

Occasionally the executioners themselves fell foul of the gore. In August 1792 Gabriel, Charles-Henri Sanson's younger son and apprentice executioner, slipped on the blood-soaked scaffold while exhibiting the head of a victim. He fell from the high platform and was mortally injured. The scaffold was later equipped with a rail to prevent such an occurrence happening again. Less dramatically, the executioners voiced numerous complaints to Fouquier Tinville that their clothes were being ruined through contamination with blood. Officials complained that the machine was not properly cleaned after the executions had been completed: 'Are good citizens to be poisoned by the stench of aristocrats' blood? Are they to empest the air even after death?'

The scaffold may have been initially assembled at the Place de la Bastille but if so it was only for one day. The Bastille had symbolised the old order. For the emerging revolutionary society, the guillotine was a thoroughly modern implement, representing progress and the new order. The epitome of justice and vengeance, the guillotine was also a display item contrived through human ingenuity. It was as if the guillotine did not really kill people but rather subdued and suppressed them, moulding them into an idealistic society. Such a perceived society was impossible to attain. In reality the vision of equality and justice foundered on the misuse of the guillotine. The Revolution had begun to embrace life and death on a grand scale, diverting its full attention to terror. Of the Reign of Terror St-Just once said: 'The experience of the Terror has dulled the sense of crime as strong liquors dull the palate.' What was never dulled was the keen edge of the guillotine's blade, which St-Just would feel for himself when his time came.

By long tradition the Place de Grève was the usual site for

executions in Paris. Indeed, it was at the Grève that the scaffold was first assembled to carry out an execution by guillotine. However, during its revolutionary career the machine was moved to various other sites that the government considered more suitable for the purpose of liberating France from its old tyrannical masters. From the Conciergerie, the main prison, the distance to the scaffold was considerable and could take up to two hours. The mode of transport was a heavy and slow-moving farm cart, a tumbrel. The journey and the routes taken ensured the maximum exposure of the condemned to the assembled crowds which often shouted and cheered loudly, eager for the impending deaths of the carts' occupants.

The Place du Carrousel, later the Place de la Réunion, was another site where the guillotine was erected, but it proved to be an unpopular location with the Assembly. The machine was too close for comfort and could be seen in operation by the members of the Assembly. It was one thing to provide the judicial background for the killings – but quite another to have to watch them taking place. On 10 May 1793 the National Assembly, meeting in the Tuileries for the first time, immediately passed a resolution ordering the Paris Municipality to move the guillotine to another location. The faint-hearted members of the Council were no doubt relieved when the machine was repositioned at the Place de la Révolution, formerly known as the Place de Louis XV. To their relief the only reminder of Dr Louis's progeny was the roar of a distant crowd. The guillotine remained at the Place de la Révolution for the next thirteen months. The Place de la Révolution was chosen by the revolutionary Tribunal in order that the guillotine's victims should receive maximum exposure and that they should be executed within a short distance from the Convention. All political offenders were given the dubious honour of being sent to their deaths at the Place de la Révolution.

The final location of the guillotine during the revolution was at the Place du Trône. Sanson's tumbrels would leave the Conciergerie and cross the Pont au Change, circling around the Hôtel de Ville, where Robespierre would eventually be captured, before being sentenced to death by the Convention that he once ruled with such oratorical expertise. The tumbrels headed out from the rue St-Antoine to the Barrière de Vincennes and the Trône, a two-hour journey undertaken by as many as sixty victims of the Terror each day. The guillotine and the executioners were never short of work.

The Place du Trône appeared to be a far more practical site for the guillotine, avoiding the disadvantages apparent at the previous locations. At the Place de la Révolution, soil and hay surrounding the scaffold became saturated with blood that poured in torrents from the jaws of the machine. Blood-stained footprints could be traced for a considerable distance into the streets leading from the square. It was after the celebrations of the Festival of the Supreme Being on 8 June 1794 (or the 25th Prairial of Year Two) that the guillotine arrived at the Trône. Its arrival coincided with a draconian edict known as the Law of 22 Prairial, effected two days after the Festival. Again demonstrating the insecurity of the authorities, the new law ordained that the revolutionary Tribunal could pronounce only one of two verdicts against those tried as the enemies of the state: acquittal or death upon the guillotine. No more than two days after the picturesque pageant of the Supreme Being, when France dedicated itself to Calm and Serene Wisdom, the Reign of Terror reached its peak. The new law of acquittal or death ensured that the guillotine's appetite would be more than satisfied.

The guillotine was now assembled at the Trône in expectation of a relentless purge of the nation's enemies. To address the problems associated with the copious amounts of blood expected to be spilled, a large trench – big enough to hold approximately 1,350 gallons – was dug below the scaffold. It was expected that the trench would easily contain both the blood from the victims and the water used to clean the machine, but in fact this great tank so quickly filled up with blood that it polluted the atmosphere. The Section Commissary was required to fill in the trench and dig another even deeper one to reach a suitable soil stratum into which the blood could eventually be absorbed. The guillotine and the new trench remained at the Trône until 9 Thermidor, or the end of July 1794. In just six weeks the guillotine had devoured some 230 victims every week.

The Reign of Terror can be divided into two separate phases. Initially it ran from March 1793 until 10 June 1794, when the Law of Prairial was enacted. Within Paris, in the span of eleven months while the guillotine was operative at the Place de la Révolution, some 1,251 souls perished beneath the blade. The second phase lasted only a short time, from 10 June to 27 July 1794, when Maximilien Robespierre was finally toppled from power. Astonishingly, the second phase of the Terror claimed the lives of 1,376 people. All executions decreed by the General Council took place in daylight hours. The guillotine had made all of this possible. The revolutionary Tribunal would have been unable to perform its functions and duties as it did without the ruthless efficiency of the guillotine. Performing all these executions manually would have taken much longer and, as Sanson had already indicated, would not have been a practical proposition.

Courage, virtue and innocence all produced their own heroes on the scaffold. The mobs watching the incessant executions regarded each day's activities as little more than theatrical entertainment. The scaffold was the stage and the condemned became the actors. The only prop was the guillotine. Each day's performance followed a set pattern: first, the arrival of the victims in the tumbrels, leading on to the main act as the condemned one by one climbed the steep steps, directed by Sanson, and the final bow as they were tipped into oblivion on the *bascule*. The audience cheered as another fine performance came to an end. The phlegmatic appearance of the majority of the victims reflected the crowd's unemotional attitude towards the carnage that ensued each day, but there were exceptions. Had all the victims of the blade behaved as Madame du Barry, then the good humour of the watching crowds would doubtless have faded. Madame du Barry, who loved life so much and showed so much compassion to the poor, was dragged into the waiting tumbrel screaming and fighting for her life. She called out to all whom she could see, protesting her innocence and begging them to save her; on her arrival at the scaffold her cries of horror and despair could be heard streets away. Sanson and three assistants had to force the distressed woman up the steps and carry her towards the guillotine. Still screaming, she was strapped to the *bascule* and it was the blade that finally silenced her. Madame du Barry could not accept the imminence of her death or that the people would allow her to be sacrificed in such a way. As she died the watching mob fell silent, their consciences pricked for perhaps the first time.

Madame du Barry's manner of death was very unusual. More typical was the behaviour of the aristocratic Colonel Vaujour. Condemned by the Tribunal, he casually asked what time the ceremony would take place. 'At two o'clock,' came the reply. The colonel retorted matter-of-factly: 'That's a pity; it is my usual dinner hour, but never mind, I shall just have to dine a little earlier.' He at once ordered several dishes, and when the fatal time arrived he had not yet finished dining. 'I shall just have a little more!' he said to Sanson, who had come to fetch him. Then he added: 'But never mind, let us be away.' As the tumbrel made its slow way to the guillotine, some women in the street shouted abuse at him. 'It is my fate,' said the indefatigable Vaujour, 'to be insulted by such riff-raff to my very last hour.' It was such displays of indomitable sang-froid and blatant courage that made the executioner's job so much easier and also allowed the mob to accept the large numbers of executions that occurred each day.

The Place de la Révolution, as the main site for the guillotine, was generally avoided by the Deputies of the Convention. Perhaps the reason was obvious; had not twenty-one of their contemporaries from the 'Plains' of the Assembly, the Girondins, been swallowed up by the 'Mountain'? The Girondins had been responsible for setting up the machinery of government that allowed the Terror to take its form. Now it had been forced to submit to the Jacobin supremacy that had purged the Convention. Twenty-one of the principal Girondin deputies and their associates met their end.

The Tribunal hated to be robbed of its vengeance. The Girondist Charles Valazé was arrested and while in prison committed suicide to escape the guillotine. None the less his corpse was propped up in the tumbrel alongside his living companions and transported to the scaffold. On reaching the Place de la Révolution, his lifeless body was carried up to the machine by two assistant executioners and the cadaver promptly guillotined. Jacobin justice had prevailed even in death. Forty minutes later Vigie, the last of the batch, was strapped to the *bascule*.

Unlike other members of the Convention, Robespierre had no qualms about the 'People's Avenger'. He lived in the Maison Duplay on the rue St-Honoré, a short distance from the Place de la Révolution. His walks to the entrance of the Champs-Elysées took him directly past the scaffold. Responsible for the deaths of many of his enemies, he was also instrumental in the saving of many lives too, if it suited his purpose. On entering the Place de la Révolution, Robespierre, always a solitary man, would stop and stare at the guillotine. His cruelty had been the prime mover of the Terror and he was by now fanatical in the political sphere. His sense of reason was sadly warped. Unlike the other deputies he seems not to have felt the least revulsion for the terrifying implement, which everyone else greatly feared. Perhaps Robespierre felt some empathy at the sight of the guillotine's proud and symmetrical structure, a fearsome presence like himself. He would stare at the machine, its sinister shape covered by a tarpaulin protecting it from the elements. Beyond the guillotine he could see the terraces of the Tuileries, close to the statue of the Goddess of Fame, a favourite spot for onlookers watching the executions, as the terraces overlooked the scaffold. He could see the pedestal of the statue of Louis XV, now surmounted by a statue of liberty, and what had once been the quarters of the Swiss Guard but was now a restaurant. In deference to the machine it was called the Tavern of the Guillotine, and on the back page of each day's menu was a list of names: the day's victims.

Unknown to Robespierre, in a matter of a few short months the Thermidor Convention would shout him down and overwhelm his followers, removing the opportunity for political riposte. They would recall the deaths of the Dantonists, an outrageous attack on liberty and free speech. The Convention would order the arrests of Robespierre and his henchmen. In defence of their own necks, they would condemn the Jacobins and send them to their deaths in the footsteps of the Girondins.

It is a strange irony that the death of the revolutionary icon Jean-Paul Marat, stabbed in his bath by Charlotte Corday, who hoped by her actions to bring an end to the bloodshed, heralded a new era in which the revolutionary wheel would turn once again on its axis and begin to consume its inventors. Marat was assassinated in July 1793, and by July 1794 all of the famous names born of the Revolution were extinct. The colourful personalities and the dull, the extremists, the moderates, the intellectual, the ordinary, the ruthless, the mad, the emotional; all were dead, consumed by the impersonal force of the guillotine.

Was the guillotine an insult to the victim's humanity? Could the trauma experienced by the victim's immediate family be expunged after the high days of the Revolution? In an attempt to come to terms with their loss, the survivors attended lavish dances – nicknamed Victims' Balls – held in remembrance of their relatives. They danced the night away with scarlet ribbons tied about their necks to represent the mark of the guillotine's blade. Admission to these soirées was eagerly sought after, and people even forged documents to 'prove' that a relative had died on the guillotine. Participants greeted each other with a nod of the head out of respect to their guillotined parents, brothers or sisters. The Thermidor cleansing had been the final period of the Revolution. Soon a city stifled by fear would return to life. In this paradoxical dance of death, execution and the fears surrounding it were ritualised. It allowed survivors and the families of victims of the Terror to come to terms with the guillotine and the suffering it had caused.

6

Justice and Retribution

'Look, traitors, and tremble: it will never rest until you have all perished.' Thus read the caption on an engraving of the guillotine in the Year Two, entitled *The Avenging Sword of the Republic* by J.B. Louivion. The blade of the guillotine shown in the engraving has an oblique edge. The machine tested at Bicêtre was the same one that was used to execute Pelletier, its first victim, after being fitted with the improved blade described by Dr Guillotin as 'bevelled'. The balance of probability is that no other form or shape of blade was used after the Bicêtre tests. Indeed, when guillotines were supplied to the French provinces in 1792 each device was accompanied by a sketch showing the traditional sloping blade – the hallmark of the guillotine. But Henri Sanson, in a letter to a fellow executioner based at Liège, stated in 1811: 'As to the shape of the axe, it is not fixed and everyone makes it as he thinks best.' This confusing statement suggests that guillotines used in the provinces until the mid-nineteenth century could have had blades that were convex, concave, scythe-shaped, sword-shaped or oblique.

Some nineteenth-century prints show peculiar scythe-shaped knives. Similar designs can also be seen on toy and model guillotines, such as those located in some French museums. The authenticity of these drawings is not generally admitted, so we are left with a reasonable assumption that no blades other than those of modern design were ever used on the original machine. There may have been certain cosmetic changes to guillotines, but none to the detriment of its underlying design features. The early days of the scarlet machine were of course its heyday: it was modern, fast and efficient, but, perhaps more than this, it was fashionable. Fashion ruled in Paris then as now. If the blade of the Paris machine was oblique, then that was the style for others to follow.

The machine belonging to the provincial Jacobin extremist Javogues was publicly auctioned in 1909 and it was noted that the uprights were crowned by carvings of revolutionary Phrygian bonnets. Such little artistic touches tell us more about the individual designer than do any design features of the guillotine itself. It is unfortunate that no description remains of the prototype Bicêtre machine. Its appearance can only be assumed from the information given in Dr Louis's specification, which may have been altered during construction. Similarly, we have no details of the altered implement used to execute the king and queen. All that remains are a few rather unreliable drawings, showing a good deal of artistic licence.

After the king's execution the guillotine was returned to the Place du Carrousel. It may have been replaced by another machine in April 1793, though this is doubtful. It is more likely that improvements were made to the existing model by fitting copper-lined grooves to the uprights, as per the original specification. The final destination of the regicidal guillotine remains a mystery, though it may have found its way to the French colonies.

The penal settlement of French Guiana, which included Devil's Island, was commonly known as the 'dry guillotine'. As convicts condemned to banishment there approached the islands from the sea, they were greeted by a chilling sight. Upon the highest summit of the island called du Salut, clearly visible from about fifteen miles distance, stood a guillotine. Its presence was intended to remind the prisoners of their fate should they stray from the rules. The executioner on the islands was always a nominated convict. The best known and most hated of all was Isidore Hespel, 'the Jackal', whose own life ended beneath the blade of the guillotine in 1923. The machine was referred to as the winch. Was this guillotine the very same Parisian machine that Sanson used to execute the king and queen during the Revolution? The author of the rumour, M. le Roux, desired that this guillotine should be preserved as an historical artefact and returned to France to be placed within the Carnavelet museum in Paris. M. le Roux also stated that the implement was still operative in 1891.

Another questionable story about the Bicêtre machine was related by the Count de Reiset:

> I was informed by the Count O'Mahony that whilst he was at the town of Auch some years ago, he was caught in a severe storm. The Count took refuge under the covered entrance of an isolated house on the town's outskirts. He sat down on some pieces of timber that had been stored beneath an outer stairway in the courtyard of the house. On returning to his family, he explained what had happened and [described] the place he had sheltered in during the storm. His cousin and host Madame Marignan listened with interest to his story and told him, 'Dear cousin, it was the courtyard of the executioner that you took refuge in. The wood you mention is a part of Louis XVI's scaffold. After the King's death, lots were drawn to decide which town should possess the scaffold and it fell to the town of Auch.' The Count, her cousin, was surprised to learn that he had rested upon parts of the very machine that had been used to execute the King.

This story may be true but no documents exist to vouch for its authenticity.

A third story relates to Nicolas Roch, executioner from 1872 until 1879. Some fourteen years after his death, his widow Madame Roch claimed to know the whereabouts of the blade of the guillotine used to execute the king. She contacted M. Dubois, a private collector from Brussels who twenty years or so earlier had purchased a guillotine from her husband. She now offered him for sale a quantity of artefacts including a blade, reputedly the very one that was used to decapitate the king and queen. Nicolas Roch had apparently inherited the items from his predecessor M. Heindreicht, executioner from 1847 until 1872. Louis Deibler, the then national executioner of France, had laid claim to the artefacts as a right of office, but was unwilling to pay Madame Roch for these important items. When she refused to hand them over, Deibler complained to the Minister of Justice, and Madame Roch was ordered to hand over the items and the blade for safekeeping in the national archives. As Madame Roch explained to M. Dubois, 'The State also refused to pay for the items so I informed the authorities that I did not possess them and did not know what my husband had done with them.'

Although there is no conclusive evidence that the blade in her possession was 'the' blade, M. Dubois was more than satisfied with her explanation and was quite happy to make the purchase. Did he really get what he wanted? Probably not. Thirty-nine years earlier Clément-Henri Sanson, the last of the Sanson family of executioners, sold an item to a M. Joseph Tussaud. His story is of interest and of some importance. Clément-Henri Sanson was the grandson of the Great Sanson, the officially appointed executioner at the time of the Revolution. The family had been executioners since the seventeenth century. Though officially appointed in 1840, Clément had been engaged in the trade of quality executing long before that, assisting his own father Henri. Clément had therefore been apprentice to the best, since his grandfather and father had been operative during the years of the Terror. The executioner's residence was often visited by curious-minded tourists who wished to see and learn more about the dread machine which was then kept and maintained at the home of the executioner.

The gracious Sansons always made visitors welcome to their home for a conducted tour, and for a modest fee the guillotine would be assembled and operated, slicing through the necks of straw dummies. For a greater fee one could purchase a live sheep for execution! Sanson found it strange that young ladies always appeared to be the most fascinated by the fearful instrument of justice. On one occasion a group of such tourists called upon Henri Sanson and his son at their residence. The father, mother and three daughters were all welcomed by the executioner and escorted to a storeroom where the guillotine had been assembled. The machine was operated several times, slicing through straw necks to the delight and applause of the three young ladies. One of the daughters, however, was not entirely satisfied with the show and began to question Sanson senior on the ritual that accompanied an execution. The *'toilette'* was then explained to her in detail. Still not satisfied, she asked in what way the condemned was secured to the machine. Sanson was in the middle of his explanation when the young lady interrupted him and asked to be bound to the *bascule*. With her father's consent the executioner tied her arms and feet with cord and strapped her to the plank. 'That's not all,' she insisted. 'Please continue!' Sanson tipped the perpendicular plank and victim to the horizontal and propelled her into the jaws of the guillotine, the blade being in position and ready for its rapid descent. The *lunette* was secured about her neck, holding her tight to the block. At this juncture, after a pause, the young lady was finally satisfied. Sanson later described what had happened: 'I quite thought for a moment that she was going to say, "That's not all, make the knife fall"!'

Victor Hugo, who later recounted this tale, also stated that Sanson had informed him that the knife that decapitated the king was sold as scrap iron along with all the other worn-out blades, though people would not accept this as a fact. Alexandre Dumas senior, however, was told something quite different.

Clément-Henri had been born with all the advantages that a potential executioner could wish for. In addition to his own pedigree, his wife was the daughter of a provincial headsman named Charles Desmorets. Executioners always married into the families of other executioners, as finding a bride from outside their ignoble profession was almost impossible on account of the prejudice and stigma associated with their work. For the executioners such prejudice was hard to accept since they saw themselves merely as an extension of the parameters of law, order and justice. No executioner ever condemned a man to die upon the guillotine. This right was reserved for the judges and yet their names were never dishonoured, nor were they ostracised or held in contempt because of their decisions.

Clément had no son to continue his distinguished family line, though he did have a daughter, who, breaking with convention, had married a Parisian doctor. When an acquaintance disparagingly expressed surprise at such an unlikely union, the sharp-witted Clément made an interesting analogy: 'Look at things a little more dispassionately; a surgeon often has to sacrifice a gangrenous part of a body in order to save the whole. If a social body has a diseased member would it not be reasonable to rid society of that too?' The guest thought for a moment, reflecting on the similarities, and replied, 'I would like you to realise that there is a considerable difference between two such operations.' The ever-quick Clément replied, 'Oh yes indeed, Monsieur, but only in the size of the knives!'

Clément-Henri was not without his faults; he was a spendthrift and indulged himself in gambling and womanising, and could be best described as a bit of a rake. His self-indulgence also included collecting expensive antiques. In his defence, perhaps these distractions helped him to take his mind off his profession. In fact it was rumoured that his occupation positively disagreed with him and at times made him physically ill. His hobbies and distractions proved to be very costly and what resources he had were soon squandered. Not even the frequent and impromptu visits by the ever-curious tourists to the home of the Sansons in the rue des Marais was enough to offset Clément's outgoings. As creditors clamoured for their money from the practically bankrupt executioner, the last of the Sansons was for a while detained in a debtors' prison, where no doubt his profession remained a secret.

On being released, and in dire need of immediate funds, Clément-Henri committed the great folly of pawning his guillotine, the very machine currently used for executions. That once mighty instrument was now debased by its very own servant. But Sanson also possessed another machine, no longer used and much older than his current one. This older machine was of particular interest – a machine that was perhaps unique. It was sheer bad luck for Clément that before he had time to accumulate sufficient funds to redeem the pawned guillotine, the Procureur Général ordered an execution to take place. Sanson now had to beg his creditor to release the guillotine for one day. The pawnbroker knew only too well why his customer needed it and with true abolitionist spirit refused to release the imprisoned guillotine.

There was nothing that could be done except to confess and admit his folly to the authorities. A furious and embarrassed government department official redeemed Sanson's pledge and freed the machine. On completion of the execution Clément-Henri Sanson, not surprisingly, was dismissed from his office in 1847, bringing to an end an executing dynasty. Clement had served in the official post of executioner for a mere seven years and his departure meant a new Monsieur de Paris would have to be appointed. The title 'Monsieur de Paris' was the colloquial term used to describe the executioner of Paris. In years gone by great gatherings took place at the Sanson residence in Paris. The many brothers of the great Sanson were also executioners and it was easier for their servants and valets to refer to each one by the town he served – M. de Paris, M. de Reims, M. de Montpellier, M. de Tours and so on. After 1870 all executions became the responsibility of a national executioner, but the nickname 'M. de Paris' remained throughout each successive executioner's career, as did the more derogatory title of *'bourreau'*. This slang title survived until the demise of the guillotine. The use of the word was prohibited as far back as 1681 because it was considered uncomplimentary, and anyone overheard using the term was subject to a fine. However, the term persisted and was commonly used into the twentieth century. The word itself is quite meaningless and originated in about 1260. It was derived from a cleric named Richard Borel who had been granted an estate called Bellencombre on condition that he hang the condemned thieves of the Canton district. As a churchman, Borel was unwilling to take anyone's life and so in order to claim the provisions of his fief he subcontracted this duty to another man. It was customary in those days to refer to him as Le Borel, and the derivation 'boreaux' was applied to those who put the criminals to death. *Boreaux* was subsequently corrupted to *bourreau* and before the seventeenth century the word was not considered offensive. Another etymology traces the word back to the role of the knacker or '*bourrelier*' in Alsace-Lorraine, where the roles of executioner and knacker were often combined.

The unlucky Clément-Henri Sanson did not appear the slightest bit perturbed over his humiliating dismissal; in fact he probably welcomed it. Rather than tactfully withdrawing from society and changing his ways, he carried on in the same old style. At the time of his dismissal he was a mere forty-eight years of age, and he lived until he was ninety. In 1854, by which time he had been out of business for seven years, he heaped further shame on the Sanson name by pawning another family treasure – the older guillotine.

On a visit to France, Joseph Tussaud redeemed the pledge from the pawnbroker and also paid Clément a further sum to purchase the guillotine from him. It was certainly not the official machine in use at that time, which had already been confiscated by the government. It was therefore a guillotine from the private museum at the rue des Marais, and more than likely it really was what Clément had claimed – the very machine used to execute the king, the original Bicêtre guillotine!

Alexandre Dumas senior had been told by Henri Sanson, Clément's father, that this unique implement was in his possession. Joseph Tussaud had paid the substantial sum of 220 pounds for the machine, half to the pawnbroker and half to Sanson, before returning to London with his prized machine. Seventy-one years later, in 1925, fire raged through Madame Tussaud's establishment in London and the guillotine and its documents of authenticity were destroyed. Only the blade and a section of the *mouton* survived the blaze.

1 The Halifax gibbet, used in Yorkshire in the sixteenth century. From Hone's *Table Book*. (*The Mary Evans Picture Library*)

2 Guillotine – sent to Indo China (now Vietnam) early in the twentieth century. It still exists and is housed at the war crimes museum in Saigon. The machine was last used in 1960. (*Courtesy of the Gordon Anderson archives*)

3 Dr Joseph-Ignace Guillotin, proposer of the 'simple device'. Engraving by
B.L. Prévost after a design by J.M. Moreau, 1785.
(*The Mary Evans Picture Library*)

4 The Swiss guillotine. This machine demonstrates the paradox of a simple device. It is a masterpiece of eighteenth century engineering. Utilising a pendulum rope release and a head clamp which prevented the victim from withdrawing his head back into the lunette. *(Courtesy of the Gordon Anderson archives)*

5 German Fallbeil. Short and squat looking, a murder machine in Nazi dominated Germany. The heavy blade and sledge that it ran on could weigh up to 200lbs. *(Courtesy of the Gordon Anderson archives)*

6 Queen Marie-Antoinette is guillotined at the Place de la Révolution (now the Place de la Concorde). Engraved by Helman after an original by Monnet. (*The Mary Evans Picture Library*)

7 The heads of the Pollet gang. Guillotined at Béthune on 11 January 1909. They are Théophile Deroo, Canut Vromont, Auguste Pollet and Abel Pollet *(Courtesy of the Gordon Anderson archives)*

8 On 20 January 1793 Louis XVI takes leave of his family before going to the guillotine. Painting by Jean-Jacques Hauer. (*The Mary Evans Picture Library*)

9 A waxwork image of Madame Tussaud, Marie Grosholtz, at the age of twenty-four. (*The Mary Evans Picture Library*)

10 Anatole Deibler and his guillotine. The guillotines were stored at 60 bis, rue de la Folie-Regnault. *(Courtesy of the Gordon Anderson archives)*

11 Houy, convicted of one murder and admitting to eighteen others, is guillotined at Versailles after refusing breakfast but accepting a glass of Cognac. Engraving by A. Dupuy in *La Police Illustrée*, 7 October, 1883. *(The Mary Evans Picture Library)*

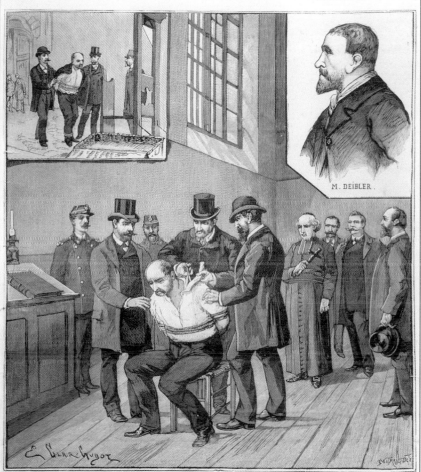

12 A typical execution scene as featured in nineteenth-century periodicals. From *Le Petit Parisien*, 15 February 1891. (*The Mary Evans Picture Library*)

13 In revolutionary Paris a cheering mob surround and salute Sainte Guillotine. The composition of the painting displays a sense of callous brutality. Käthe Kollwitz, *Die Carmagnole*, 1901. Aquatint. (*Photo AKG, London: © Staatliche Kunstsammlungen, Dresden*)

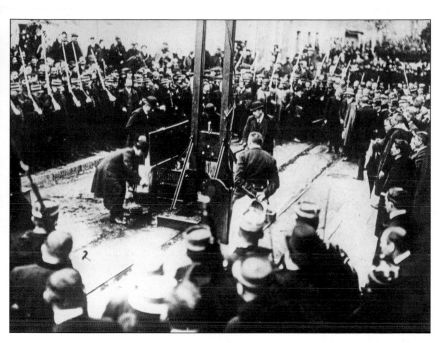

14   The execution of the 'Chauffers de la Drôme' at Valence on 22 September 1909. Louis Berruyer, Octave David and Louis Liottard were guillotined for similar crimes as the Pollet gang committed. *(Courtesy of the Gordon Anderson archives)*

15   The guillotine in Algeria. This was the modern guillotine before 1870 when the mouton, arrowhead and grab device were mounted on the other side of the apparatus. This was later altered to avoid potential damage to the lunette. *(Courtesy of the Gordon Anderson archives)*

16 The executioner's hangar at 60 bis, rue de la Folie-Regnault.
(Courtesy of the Gordon Anderson archives)

17 The author Robert Opie standing to the left of one of the miniature guillotines he made for American patron and friend Gordon Anderson.
(a trick composite photograph created by Gordon Anderson)

18 Older version of the German fallbeil. This taller machine has the design features of the French guillotines. *(Courtesy of the Gordon Anderson archives)*

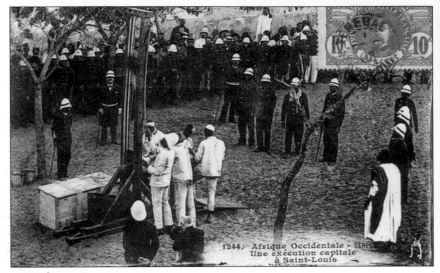

19 An execution at Senegal in the nineteenth century. This guillotine is mounted on a wheeled chassis. The blade can be seen descending in mid flight.
(Courtesy of the Gordon Anderson archives)

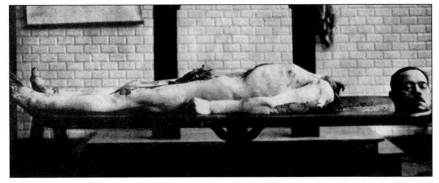

20 Executed criminal. Albert Fournier guillotined at Tours on 25 February 1920.
(Courtesy of the Gordon Anderson archives)

21 Front view of the modern guillotine about 1907. *(Courtesy of the Gordon Anderson archives)*

22 The last public execution in France. The murderer Eugène Weidmann is guillotined by Henri Desfourneaux outside the St Pierre prison at Versailles on 17 June 1939. A large crowd had waited up all night to view the spectacle. In 1981 the French government finally approved a bill to abolish the death penalty, ending nearly two centuries of the use of the guillotine. *(Courtesy of the Gordon Anderson archives)*

23 Guillotine at Fresnes Prison in 1981. Altered by André Obrecht when he was chief executioner, the blade has been widened and the braces re-fashioned and replaced. *(Courtesy of the Gordon Anderson archives)*

24 German fallbeil and scaffold. Chief executioner Franz Xavier Reichart is pictured in the middle. *(Courtesy of the Gordon Anderson archives)*

Madame Tussaud's museum had been razed to the ground and with it disappeared the answer to an intriguing mystery.

At the time of the Terror the diminutive Marie Grosholtz, later Madame Tussaud, was the companion of doctor-turned-model-maker Philippe Curtius. She was the daughter of his housekeeper, and as a child had developed a keen talent for sculpture and modelling. Dr Curtius encouraged the young Marie, combining her talents with his own. His well-known Salon de Cire allowed the public to gaze in wonder at the wax effigies of the famous personalities of the day, including the effigies of notorious criminals who had met their end at the hands of the executioner. The popularity of this new venture in modelling encouraged Curtius and Marie to open the first 'Chamber of Horrors', the Caverne des Grands Voleurs, in 1783. Marie's artistic talents came to the attention of the Princess Elisabeth, Louis XVI's sister. Marie was invited to the palace of Versailles to tell the princess about the intricacies of modelling, some nine years before the Revolution.

By the year 1792 the French Revolution was well under way and with the rising slaughter at the guillotine the numbers of suitable subjects for display in Curtius's museum on the Temple Boulevard dramatically increased. Dr Curtius, like so many others of the middle and professional classes, became caught up in the revolutionary fervour that swept through France. He was a member of the National Guard and also a staunch Jacobin. He knew personally both Danton and Robespierre, and was also acquainted with Charles-Henri Sanson.

As the Revolution progressed, Curtius and Marie made models of the heads of the guillotine's victims which were then exhibited in the Salon de Cire's annexe, the Hall of the Great Thieves. The work undertaken by the 28-year-old Marie was decidedly unpleasant but also of paramount importance, even to the point of ensuring her own fragile existence in the eye of the Terror's storm. She must have had a strong constitution. She would accompany Sanson's cart to the graveyard, where in the twilight she would identify the freshly severed heads and begin the construction of the death-masks for their eventual exhibit in the museum – unsavoury work that had to be undertaken as soon after the executions as possible. Her first task was to oil the skin so it would not dry out. A plaster mould was then taken to make the impression for modelling in wax. Fine colourings and skin textures were applied over the effigy to create the death-mask. Perhaps the high point of her career came when the National Convention ordered Dr Curtius – and thus Marie – to sculpt the death-masks of Louis XVI and later Marie-Antoinette.

Among the many others whose images graced the Chamber of Horrors were various notorious Revolutionaries, including Robespierre, St-Just, Hébert and the abominable Fouquier Tinville. Their heads were mounted upon bayonets and pikes, and placed alongside their victims, including the king and queen. The waxworks covering the period of the French Revolution proved to be, and remain today, the most popular section of the exhibition when it found its permanent home in London in 1834. It was a great loss when some of the original exhibits were destroyed by fire in 1925.

In the early 1990s visitors to Wookey Hole in the West Country, famous for its caves and subterranean rivers, would have seen a display loaned from Madame Tussaud's in London. Set up in the old papermill, which had been renovated as a working museum, the exhibit included Jean-Paul Marat lying in his bath, stabbed by the hand of Charlotte Corday; the heads and death-masks of Louis XVI and Marie-Antoinette; and the heads of Robespierre, Tinville and Madame Elisabeth, the king's sister. But the most dramatic item on display was a full-scale replica of a nineteenth-century French guillotine. This same guillotine was on display during the 1950s in Madame Tussaud's in London, though today it has been replaced with a newer version. Only a few small inaccuracies might have been noticed. The *mouton* and blade are of the type in which an iron bar projects from the heavy weight. This blade extension would normally have been supported by a pivoted blade release lever (which was missing) attached to the side of one of the uprights. Also missing was the pulley normally inserted into the top crossbar or *chapiteau* and used to haul the blade aloft. Finally this particular model would probably have been painted red rather than the existing sombre brown. Perhaps this guillotine is a copy of the machine purchased from Clément-Henri Sanson in 1854 by Joseph Tussaud, the grandson of Marie Grosholtz-Tussaud.

Clément-Henri Sanson may well be accused of having brought his family name into disrepute. His ancestors had carried out their function as executioners honourably and impartially. But Clément was not the only executioner to have his career cut short. There were others too, except in their cases the cutting short resulted in the loss of their heads. The Revolution's worst atrocities occurred not in Paris but in the provinces, where the true spirit of the Revolution was defiled. In the town of Chinon, for example, a touring circus brought more to the town than the simple delights of the carnival. At that time Chinon had no revolutionary Tribunal. Caught up in the zeal of the times, the circus established its own tribunal in the town to seek out and destroy the enemies of France. This process was copied throughout the provinces – with devastating results. As in the capital, no individual in the provinces was safe from the blade of the guillotine. The atrocities carried out by these rogue groups far outweighed those occurring in Paris. Men, women, even children and animals became the guillotine's regular diet.

At Chinon the circus clown was appointed as prosecutor – but it quickly became apparent that it was no laughing matter when this sadistic individual set about the task of settling old scores. His activities led to many innocent lives being lost. Within a year this 'flame of the Revolution', as he liked to be called, became the most hated and despised member of the community. Such power is all too easily abused, but eventually the clown himself was seized, tried and condemned to death for his nefarious activities. He too would feel the kiss of steel. To the delight and relief of the townsfolk this dreadful creature who had caused so much trauma was put back into his clown's suit, complete with big boots and baggy trousers, then paraded to the scaffold where he was promptly guillotined.

Joseph le Bon was an ex-priest and revolutionary psychopath who took the Jacobin Terror to the town of Cambrai in northern France. He dressed flamboyantly in a yellow coat, and his hat was decked with red, white and blue ostrich feathers. Le Bon erected his provincial guillotine in the centre of the town square, where many innocent victims, ordinary and harmless citizens, fell prey to his evil ways. Having abandoned his ecclesiastical vows, he did what Robespierre had demanded of all such clerics, and married. His wife was also his cousin, and her evil nature was a match for his. Both derived pleasure from watching executions. His wife knew that her debauched husband was also a womaniser, and her keenest gratification came from observing the executions of many of the young ladies who had passed through his hands. The wickedness of the Terror in Cambrai was self-evident since the members of his Tribunal consisted of le Bon, his wife, his brother-in-law and three of his uncles. Le Bon's tyrannical reign ended only when news reached Cambrai of Robespierre's downfall and execution. The wicked ex-priest fled the town but was soon hunted down and arrested. Following his own appearance before a new Government Tribunal, he was sentenced to death for his atrocities against the inhabitants of Cambrai. In 1795 the townsfolk took pleasure in seeing him lose his own head on his own guillotine.

Brief reference has already been made to Hespel (the Jackal), who was guillotined in French Guiana in 1923. René Belbenoit, a prisoner who spent fifteen years on the islands before escaping to America, witnessed his execution. Hespel was hated and despised by all the inmates. He was a murderer condemned to banishment, but on the islands he was also the camp's executioner. René Belbenoit describes the scene:

> The executioner, aided by two turnkeys, was putting the finishing touches to the guillotine. The knife was dropped to see if it was working well. Soon after, guards appeared and then the commandant. The Jackal's cell was across the courtyard; they unlocked the door and brought him out.

There were convicts grouped in a circle around the instrument; they had been brought out of the blockhouses on the other side. The order 'Kneel down' was barked and every convict hastily knelt down.

When Hespel found himself before the guillotine, he stopped and addressed the executioner – the man now at the knife had been his former assistant. 'You see, now the executioner becomes the executed! My predecessor also at last gave his head to the widow. Be careful, someday your turn will come.' After a slight pause, he saluted the executioner and added, 'Do it neatly, mon-enfant, just like I showed you the job should be done.'

In a few seconds the Jackal's head lay in the basket. 'That's it' cried out the men in the house when they heard the knife clatter. There were whistles and catcalls; they hated him, every one of them, for he had cut off thirty heads.

When the guillotine first appeared in the late eighteenth century, it was state-of-the-art equipment and its very efficiency set it apart. It may have been extremely bloody when put to use, but it was considered quick, efficient and relatively painless. It was publicly and politically acceptable because of the powerful concept of equality, both in life and also in death for those who transgressed the rule of law. The search for a method of execution that accords with society's perceptions of decency has continued wherever capital punishment is practised. The debate on the means, the efficacy and the justification for capital punishment will doubtless continue as long as the practice of judicial execution holds sway, but in revolutionary France the guillotine was believed to be the perfect means.

It may have been the 'perfect' machine, but even in the guillotine's early days some people felt it was not fast enough. During the Terror there were so many executions to be carried out that the standard guillotine could not keep pace with the numbers. A few inventive but warped minds suggested the construction of a new machine, a nine-bladed monster. There were even rumours that such a device was already under construction. M. Guillot, who was blessed with a most appropriate name, was linked with the invention and construction of the new device. Thankfully the nightmarish machine never materialised and soon afterwards the inventive Guillot was arrested for the crime of forgery. Found guilty, he was quite efficiently guillotined on the existing standard model.

Meanwhile the military commissioners at Bordeaux, under the supervision and leadership of one M. Lacombe, had constructed or at least planned a four-bladed machine. Fortune smiled on the citizens of Bordeaux, since once again this product of over-ambitious minds bent on maximum destruction was never recorded as seeing active service. If ever such a device was constructed, then it no longer exists. Lacombe's efforts were rewarded by being guillotined on the 14 August 1794!

The first guillotine differed somewhat from its latter-day counterparts. It was undoubtedly a taller machine, standing almost 18ft high, and was of much heavier construction. By the early 1800s, some twenty or so years after its debut, it had permanently adopted the design features still familiar to us today. Over the following one hundred years only minor alterations were made to its basic structure. Standing a little over 14½ft high (4.5cm); the two uprights with brass lined grooves were spaced 14½in (37cm) apart. The visible lengths of the posts stood a fraction under 12ft high. The oblique razor-edged blade weighed 16lb (7kg) and was attached to a heavy iron weight (the *mouton*) by three large steel bolts each weighing 2lb (1kg). Affixed on the outer edge of the *mouton* were four small wheels, two on each side located one above the other, to increase the speed of the drop. The *mouton* had a mass of some 70lb (30kg) and was hauled aloft by means of a rope over a single large pulley attached to the top crossbar. The *bascule*, a hinged and tilting plank, could be swiftly tipped from the perpendicular to the horizontal plane and slid forward on two rollers towards the uprights. The *lunette*, each half with a bevelled semi-circle cut into it locked the victim's head between the uprights.

Justice and Retribution

The guillotine's accessories included a receptacle to receive the head, and a lined body basket. A three-sided screen or baffle was placed on the head side of the *lunette* to impede the gush of blood that spurted from the corpse. The machine was mounted upon a heavy cross-shaped base with front and side supports and weighed in total 1278lb (580kg). On being released from its ready position, the blade descended a distance of almost 7½ft (2.25m) in less than three-quarters of a second, striking the shrinking neck beneath and instantly decapitating the victim at the third or fourth cervical vertebra. The wheels attached to the side edges of the *mouton* were reputedly the last improvements to be made to the modern guillotine, and were installed after 1899 by Anatole Deibler.

There is evidence that refutes the assumption that Anatole Deibler installed the wheels onto the *mouton*. They were in fact in place as early as 1813. A guillotine complete with a wheeled mouton accompanied Napoleon's army to Germany. The machine now resides in the Nuremburg museum but it is not on display.

7

The Cemetery

It was almost nightfall before Sanson's cart departed from the Place de la Révolution, turning out of the cobbled square into the rue Royale. Only a few hours earlier the square had been packed with crowds of people watching the guillotine relentlessly removing heads at the rate of one every minute, but now all seemed quiet and deserted. Only the servants of the guillotine remained, still at work after the day's operations, cleaning and brushing down the scaffold. Except for the executioners, there was little activity, save for some revellers heading towards the gardens of the Tuileries and the muted sounds of laughter emanating from the 'Tavern of the Guillotine'.

The day had been hot and dry, yet the scaffold and the machine were soaked with a mixture of blood and water, the result of washing down the apparatus after an exhausting day's work. The guillotine had to be dried off as much as possible before it was covered with its large black tarpaulin. Certainly it deserved its nickname 'The Widow', standing alone in the square all clad in black.

Sanson, by order of the General Council of the Commune, had removed the blade of the device and secured it in a wooden box for safekeeping overnight. The next morning the guillotine would be reassembled for the new batch of customers. By August 1793 the machine was permanently located in the Place de la Révolution, where, despite the efforts made every day to clean the machine and the scaffolding of blood, no scrubbing could erase the red stain beneath and around the scaffold. The soil spread beneath the great ten-stepped platform was repeatedly saturated with human blood, and bloody footprints could be followed as far as the rue Bourgogne before fading away. This was a somewhat distressing problem to the citizens of Paris, who were continually preoccupied with the spread of pestilence and plague.

Soon, following the Festival of the Supreme Being on 25 Prairial of Year Two of the Revolution, during the celebrations for which even the guillotine was adorned in costume, the whole ghastly apparatus would be removed to the Barrière du Trône-Renversé, there to carry on the objectives of the unholy Terror. Meanwhile the shrouded widow would continue to operate in the Place de la Révolution, its tall frame scarring the graceful lines of the avenue of the Tuileries.

In the heavily laden tumbrel Sanson transported his load of decapitated bodies and their separated heads to their final destination some half a mile distant, the cemetery of the Madeleine in the Ville-l'Evêque. Blood was still dripping from the corpses on to the roadway. The wheels on the tumbrel were somewhat smaller than those of the original heavy hay-carts, and though they were adequate on hard-surfaced roads they later proved troublesome when the authorities selected a new cemetery at the end of the faubourg called Picpus for the large batches of victims guillotined at the Trône-Renversé. At Picpus the narrow wheels of the tumbrels sank into the soft soil here, quickly becoming bogged down.

In due course the Revolutionaries, themselves victims of the guillotine, would join the grim procession to the cemetery. Eventually, the Terror itself was subdued after the arrest and death of Robespierre and his disciples. The guillotine was removed from the Trône and reassembled at the Place de la Révolution. After a final bloodletting in which the Thermidor Convention purged itself of the radical extremists, the guillotine was removed from the square and with its departure the public's fears began at last to dissipate. The city could sense liberty and, freed from tyranny, its people could go about their business in relative safety. Before his execution Georges Danton exclaimed: 'The revolutionary Tribunal! I ask forgiveness for it from God and men.' It was certainly in need of forgiveness for in a little over two years, from April 1793 until July 1795, Dr Guillotin's device had taken nearly 3,000 lives within the city of Paris.

* * *

Ninety minutes passed before the now empty cart departed from the Madeleine cemetery, retracing its journey down the rue Royale. Within the cemetery the bodies of the former aristocrats had been placed at the bottom of a large trench. The heads were also tumbled into this trench, falling like melons from wicker baskets, and all the stiffening mass of desecrated humanity was covered with quicklime. There were no markers or gravestones to be seen; such people were destined to rest in anonymity. In death they had no memorial and their names survived only in the lists of the guillotined maintained by the executioner. Sanson's final task of the day was to return to the Conciergerie to report to the members of the Tribunal.

The disposal of the victims' remains took place in different cemeteries according to the various sites where the guillotine was operative. By far the greatest number of the victims within Paris were beheaded at the Place de la Révolution, including the king and queen. More than one thousand bodies were subsequently interred in the cemetery of the Madeleine in the rue de la Ville-l'Evêque, formerly a garden owned by Benedictine nuns. During July 1794 sixteen Carmelite nuns from Compiègne were sentenced to die on the guillotine. In their final hours they were rejoined by a runaway nun, who, hearing of her sisters' condemnation, had decided to return to them and share their fate. The nuns were taken to the scaffold and lined up at the foot of the steps singing the 'Salve Regina'. Not one showed any fear. As Sanson beckoned each one forward in turn, the chorus became quieter and quieter until there were no voices left to be heard. The Revolutionaries' fury was not directed at monks or nuns, but was concentrated more against priests and those with royalist sympathies. But very often no distinction was made between the two groups and as a result many innocents perished, not only on the guillotine but also at the mercy of murderers and assassins who took the law into their own hands.

The revolutionary government confiscated the possessions and wealth of the Church and in the process placed the cemeteries of Paris under secular control. The cemeteries would eventually be sold after the fire of the Revolution had died down, but they were not allowed to be used again until ten years had elapsed from the last executions. In 1792 only two cemeteries, Vaugirard and Clamart, had been available for the city of Paris, but the increasing numbers of executions at that time meant that an additional site was required to accommodate the great number of bodies. As the authorities now controlled the cemeteries, they appropriated the garden at the Madeleine as the new cemetery site. In January 1792 the Republic instructed that a large trench some 10 feet deep was to be dug within the garden, and a large deposit of quicklime was ordered. On 20 January 1793 the body of King Louis XVI was taken to the cemetery for burial. The king's remains were given a brief burial service. The Abbé Reinard recited the prayers for the dead over the king's remains, watched by a silent crowd of onlookers. Perhaps they could scarcely believe that the headless corpse before them constituted the mortal remains of their king. Louis was buried in a common grave, his body still dressed in the clothes he had worn on his journey to the guillotine – grey breeches and a white but now heavily bloodstained waistcoat. His hat was a small tricorn, to which had been pinned a national cockade. His shoes had been removed before burial and were missing. Louis's eyes remained open and his head had not yet taken on the waxy pallor of death. With only an open box for a coffin, the corpse was laid with the head placed between the legs. After this rude sarcophagus had been lowered into the pit, the remains were covered with quicklime. The Madeleine cemetery would serve as the burial ground for those who had been guillotined until March 1794.

It is interesting to note that the Parisians, who evidently had no qualms about the use of the guillotine, were rather more particular about the disposal of the bodies. People who lived close to the burial grounds were very alarmed about the potential spread of disease from the corpses of the executed. In fact there was very little danger because of the ample use of quicklime, but nevertheless the public anxiety persisted, despite assurances from the Government that there was no risk. The widespread anxiety eventually prompted the authorities to select another burial site in the rue des Errancis, known as the cemetery of Mousseaux. The new site became operative on 25 March 1794 and the guillotined were buried here until 10 June that year. However, all the deceased were taken first to the Madeleine even after March 1794 and often they remained there for a number of days before being transported at night to the new site, now commonly called the Errancis cemetery. The authorities insisted on this clandestine activity to allay further public concerns over the potential for epidemics breaking out in the area of the new cemetery.

When the guillotine was moved to the Barrière du Trône-Renversé, another site was needed closer to the spot where the executions were carried out. It would have to be large enough to accommodate the great batches of victims sent to their deaths at the hands of Fouquier Tinville. The location chosen was the cemetery at the church of Sainte Marguerite. This cemetery was already overcrowded with 'normal' burials, which were happily tolerated by the local inhabitants, but the bodies of the guillotined provoked further unrest and another place had to be found.

Picpus was chosen. Formerly a convent garden belonging to the Augustinian canonesses, this site had also been 'nationalised' by the government following the suppression of the Church. Large trenches were again ordered to be dug and the necessary supply of quicklime was purchased. In an attempt to avoid confrontation, the authorities never openly stated where the burial grounds were located. Everyone – men, women and even children – knew where the places of execution were, and yet very few were aware of the places of interment, not even the close relations of the guillotined.

The Cemetery

The Madeleine cemetery was isolated and peaceful, lying within an area of grassed meadowland. The rue d'Anjou ran along one side, with the rue l'Arcade on the opposite side. Hardly any people lived close to the cemetery, which was largely why the authorities had chosen it. The risk of an epidemic arising from the burials was also reduced.

The king's burial was accompanied by prayers for his departed soul, though the queen, who had been so despised by the people, did not receive this Christian service. Nor did the majority of the guillotined. Worse still, when the number of bodies outweighed the efforts of the men selected to bury them, it often happened that the corpses were left lying exposed in the pit for a day or two, their bodies shown none of the normal respect for the dead.

In Paris it used to be the custom that the clothing of the victims became the property of the executioner, but this privilege was now claimed by the Republic. This involved a substantial loss of income for the executioners, who had previously either sold the clothes or used them to replace their own, frequently ruined in the course of their occupation. Now the deceased were rudely stripped and their clothing sorted into separate batches of trousers, coats and shoes, etc. Rinsed clean, usually in the river, the clothing was then distributed to the hospitals and refuges to aid the poor. The naked bodies of the victims were then simply thrown into the pit without decency, one on top of another, before being covered with quicklime.

At the end of the Revolution M. Descolozeaux, an anti-Revolutionist and royalist sympathiser, managed to purchase the Madeleine cemetery. He and a relative had been obliged to maintain a low profile during the years of the Terror, but they endeavoured to observe and keep notes on the activities around the cemetery. They carefully recorded the burials of the king and queen, and when it was safe to do so planted weeping willow trees near the spot where they lay. For more than twenty years the remains of the king and queen rested in the little cemetery of the Madeleine. Then in 1815, when Napoleon was in exile on the island of Elba and King Louis XVIII sat upon the throne of France, M. Descolozeaux told the king his precious information. The king ordered a thorough search to be conducted at the Madeleine and in January 1815 the bodies of Louis XVI and his queen were located. Twenty-two years to the day since Louis XVI had gone to the guillotine, his remains and those of the queen, both sealed in lead-lined coffins, were transported in a hearse to the vaults of the cathedral of St Denis. Here they would finally lie in peace amid their Bourbon ancestors. Watched by a silent multitude, the extensive procession passed through the streets of Paris along the very same route that Louis had taken to the scaffold many years previously.

Louis XVIII, who had but few years of life remaining to him, commissioned a chapel to be built in memory of Louis and Marie-Antoinette. It was constructed upon the site of the Madeleine, and by the time it was completed France had a new king, Charles X. Although the remains of the king and queen now lay at rest in St Denis, a mixture of soil and quicklime that had adhered to their bodies was sealed within a marble coffin and retained within the chapel. Inside this building, called La Chapelle Expiatoire, Louis and Marie-Antoinette are immortalised in fine marble statues. The kneeling king is directed towards heaven by an angel, a symbol of the sad Abbé Edgeworth who remained with the king until the last second. Beneath the statue in letters of gold are printed the king's last will and testament, penned upon the day of his death: 'Let my Son know, never to seek to avenge my death, tell him to think only of his fellow citizens.' Interestingly he referred not to his subjects but to his fellow citizens! He went on to ask forgiveness from his wife for the unhappiness she had reaped because of him and he forgave those who were about to murder him. Louis and Marie-Antoinette would never know of the frail little Dauphin's terrible destiny, slowly killed through the actions of inattentive and evil men, who feared that the Revolution might be undone if a Capet were to live.

A statue of the queen stands opposite Louis. She is clothed in a long flowing dress and her face gazes towards the cross. Her crown, symbolic of the root cause of all her misery, lies at her feet, partly hidden by the billowing folds of her gown. Beneath her statue are the words of her last letter, penned by her own hand in her bleak cell within the Conciergerie, and addressed to Madame Elisabeth, Louis's sister (see Appendix 4). On the day of Marie-Antoinette's death, this letter was handed to Fouquier Tinville, who in turn passed it to Robespierre. Cruelly he hid the letter beneath his mattress in the Maison Duplay and so the tragic Madame Elisabeth never received it. The letter was discovered among Robespierre's personal effects the day after his execution by a member of the Convention named Curtois. He kept the letter for twenty years, finally offering it to Louis XVIII to bargain for a pardon in atonement for his revolutionary indiscretions. The king took the letter from Curtois and ordered his banishment to Belgium; he was never heard of again.

After much deliberation the king decided that the letter should be shown to Marie-Antoinette's daughter, the Duchesse d'Angoulême. Now a grown woman, she was the sole survivor of that melancholy royal family that lived out their last days in the Temple prison. When the duchesse saw her mother's handwriting and read her words, the memory of those last days flooded her mind and she fainted. The letter still survives, sealed in a lead-lined box and lodged in the national archives.

Today the Madeleine cemetery is a place of stillness and tranquillity, a little island of peace surrounded by the busy boulevards of Paris. It is hard to believe that a little over two hundred years ago it echoed to the sound of the wheels of the tumbrels, bearing the corpses of the guillotined to the cemetery. Manon Philipon also rests here. Better known to history as Madame Roland, she was guillotined in the same month as the queen. An inspiration to the Girondins, Madame Roland maintained her dignity throughout her protracted days of imprisonment in the Conciergerie. Her fortitude was an example to other prisoners and gave them strength to face their destiny.

Also in the chapel is the tomb of Charlotte Corday. She did not know Paris at all, and her journey there was to serve only one purpose: to rid the Revolution and humanity of a cruel man. As Corday was on her way to the guillotine on 17 July 1793, Sanson compassionately tried to obstruct her view of the machine. Turning to him she said, 'But, Monsieur, I have a right to be curious, I have never seen it before.'

In the crypt of the chapel stands a marble tombstone marking the spot where the bodies of the guillotined were originally buried. The bitter harvest that death reaped is stored in the vaults of Madeleine, the innocent lying with the guilty, the religious with the profane and the just with the cruel. Long after the harvest had been gathered, the guillotine would still remain, symbolic of what had been and what could still be.

The Madeleine cemetery was closed in 1794 as a result of overcrowding, just two weeks before the executions of Danton and his friends and colleagues. They lie elsewhere. But the Madeleine contains various well-known people who came to prominence during the Revolution: M. Vergniaud, the great public speaker and Girondist; Adam Lux, who was so inspired by Charlotte Corday's sacrifice, her countenance and her beauty that he too desired and welcomed death beneath the same blade; Philippe Egalité, the king's cousin, who voted for Louis's death; Madame du Barry, the beloved mistress of Louis XV, dragged to the guillotine screaming and pleading for her life; Hébert and his associates, an obscenity of a man who rejoiced in the fear and deaths of so many of his betters; Madame Elisabeth, the king's sister; and many more. Not everybody there was a victim of the guillotine. Also buried there are the remains of the Princess de Lamballe, the queen's friend, who was first raped and then murdered by a mob. After her death her defiled remains and head were mounted upon a pike and displayed beneath the royal apartments of the Temple.

The bodies of those guillotined at the Trône were taken to Picpus. On Tuesday 22 July 1794, St Madeleine's Day, a large batch of prisoners were preparing to leave the Conciergerie in three tumbrels. Those condemned included a mother, her daughter-in-law and her granddaughter, namely Madame la Maréchale de Noailles, Madame la Duchesse d'Ayen, daughter-in-law to the maréchale, and the Vicomtesse de Noailles, daughter of the duchesse. The vicomtesse was approximately twenty-four years old. The Abbé Carrichon, who had become a friend of this doomed family, had promised the maréchale absolution on the journey to the scaffold, but it would have to be done secretly and quietly. They would know him by his manner of dress, a dark blue coat and red waistcoat. Looking into the prison courtyard, the Abbé saw the first of the three carts being filled with the condemned. It held a total of eight ladies, one of whom was the Maréchale de Noailles. The cart moved forward to the edge of the courtyard, where it stopped. It was to be a full fifteen minutes before the remaining two carts were filled and began their long journey to the Place du Trône. The mother and daughter, in complete despair, had taken their places in the second cart. The vicomtesse was aware that her husband's parents, the Maréchal and Maréchale de Mouchy, had already made the same journey to the guillotine and that now the remainder of the family were to follow.

The Abbé Carrichon was distraught. He had followed the tumbrels through the Faubourg but had been unable to make himself seen by the Noailles family and they would soon be approaching the Trône. As the tumbrels closed in on their destination the mob's numbers had increased, swallowing him up. The tumbrels conveying the Noailles family had all but reached the Trône when suddenly and without warning a heavy storm broke. The skies opened, and howling winds and lashing rain cleared the streets of most of the mob. At this moment the abbé was at last seen by the maréchale, who raised her eyes to heaven in recognition of her silent absolution. The carts had now all reached the scaffold.

At the scaffold a strange thought entered the abbé's mind, inspired by the efficiency of the executioner and his assistants. Unlike the mob, they were not mocking or insulting to the condemned. They took care of the victims, who were carefully lined up at the base of the scaffold with their backs to the apparatus in order that they should see nothing until their moment had come. Such a quick death, the abbé thought, was at least a merciful act, but for that terrible noise when it all began. For each victim there were three crashing blows of the machine: the *bascule* falling hard upon the frame of the table, the upper section of the *lunette* slamming down about the neck of the victim, and then, almost immediately, the heavy crash and rebound of the blade. The abbé was repulsed: how could the mob so cheerfully watch people being slaughtered like this day after day?

The abbé watched his sheep being slaughtered. The maréchale was the third of the day and the first of the three ladies, Madame d'Ayen the tenth. She was followed by her daughter. In just twenty minutes fifty persons had been removed from the carts and twelve of them had been guillotined. The blood flowed continuously, seeping through the floor of the scaffold. The abbé could watch no more and with faltering steps he withdrew, becoming lost in the noisy crowds.

In 1802, when the revolutionary tempest had died down, Madame Montagu Noailles returned to France. Her first priority was to locate the grave of her mother, the Duchesse d'Ayen, and those of the rest of her family who had perished in the Place du Trône. But so anonymous were the burial places that no one was able to give her any information to aid her search. She was eventually directed to an old lady called Madame Paris, who had been a maker of fine lace before the Revolution. When Madame Noailles explained the reasons for her search, Madame Paris was reduced to tears and admitted that she knew the location of Madame Montagu's deceased relatives. She went on to tell her own story of sadness.

Madame Paris's father André was a groom and coach-driver employed by the Duc de Brissac. Her younger brother François was a servant and also a member of the National Guard. Both had been arrested and condemned by the Tribunal in July 1794, at the same time as the Noailles family. André Paris was an infirm old man who had been in employment for thirty years and yet he had been condemned. Madame Paris watched in horror as her father and young brother were both swept up by the Terror. Both were guillotined on the same day as the Noailles family at the Place du Trône-Renversé. At the end of the day, just before nightfall, she followed the tumbrels laden with bodies to a burial trench at the cemetery at Picpus.

The day after her meeting with Madame Paris, Madame Montagu journeyed to Picpus accompanied by Madame Lafayette. Together they found the little cemetery. It was surrounded by a wall and in the enclosure stood an iron cross. It was later ascertained that Picpus had been sold in July 1801 and then resold to the Princess Hohenzollern, whose brother, Frédéric III prince de Salm Kilburg, had been guillotined along with fifty-two others on 23 July 1794.

Mesdames Montagu and Lafayette eventually managed to purchase the garden of the Augustinian canonesses, and with the agreement of the Princess Hohenzollern annexed it to the ground containing the common grave. A large chapel was built there, and the names of more than 1,300 victims of the guillotine were inscribed on marble panels. In time the garden would become known as the Field of Martyrs. The tomb of General Lafayette is also there.

At the end of July 1794 the common grave at Picpus had been closed as the guillotine was removed from the Trône and returned to the Place de la Révolution. The cemetery at Errancis was then used again to accommodate the bodies of the victims, including Danton and the Dantonists, Camille Desmoulins and his wife Lucille, Robespierre and his henchmen, including St-Just, Payan, Fleuriot Lescot and numerous others. On the iron door is embossed the word 'Sleep', but one wonders whether such contentious spirits can ever be at peace.

In 1817 the tangled bones buried in the Errancis were disinterred and taken south of the Seine to the Place Denfert-Rochereau and reburied in the catacombs there. Thirty years later, in the mid-1800s, the Errancis cemetery disappeared into the pages of history. It now lies hidden forever under the streets and boulevards of the Parc Monceau and a very different Paris.

8

Dead or Alive?

The guillotine was the invention of men of science, medical professionals whose main aim in their varied careers was the preservation of life. The machine was developed to minimise the suffering of criminals whose lives were ordained to end through the judicial process. These humanitarian ideals were overturned by the excesses of the Revolution, culminating in the production of a death machine incorporating some of the first examples of 'modern' technology. No executioner was now required to strike the fatal blow. The machine, an extrapolation of justice, did the job for them, speedily and efficiently. In fact, the guillotine could be viewed as a modern surgical instrument with an operating capacity that produced a 100 per cent success rate. The machine was not without its detractors. Medical opinions concerning the guillotine reflected both extremes of the spectrum: it was efficient and humane; it was barbaric and tortuous. From the machine's early days it was to become a subject of medical controversy, posing a dilemma and raising insoluble problems.

The production of the guillotine soon gave rise to widely differing opinions concerning its efficacy within the medical profession. Some of the views expressed were diametrically opposed to those of Dr Guillotin and Dr Louis. Some people believed that, rather than inflicting a swift and merciful death, this simple device was one of the most horrific and inhumane forms of judicial murder that had ever been invented. They were devoted to a quest to prove their beliefs and to bring about the abandonment of the machine as the means of capital punishment. The controversy rumbled on throughout the reign of the guillotine into more recent times, but the use of the machine would not be abandoned until 1981.

Physiologists were to question repeatedly whether death upon the guillotine was really instantaneous, or whether there was not good evidence for the survival of consciousness and the senses for a period of time. A brief period of time perhaps, but one that was long enough for the mind to become aware of its appalling circumstances and perhaps even to face burial 'alive'. The question was an insoluble one, but the arguments dragged on. Was the machine really inflicting a quick and humane form of death, or was it barbarously inhumane, merely creating a new form of torture?

The research embarked upon by doctors and surgeons continued from the first appearance of the guillotine until the 1950s and involved some rather unethical experiments using the freshly severed heads of notorious criminals. The tests carried out to discern whether or not perception persisted after execution were hardly distinguishable from the tales of gothic horror literature such as Mary Shelley's *Frankenstein* or the history of Vlad Tepes the Impaler.

At approximately 7pm on 17 July 1793 Charlotte Corday was guillotined at the Place de la Révolution. François le Gros, an assistant executioner, lifted her severed head from the basket and paraded about the scaffold with it, as usual. Reputedly a Marat enthusiast, le Gros then sadistically struck one side of the face with his hand. The mob was strangely offended by this action and the severed head was alleged to have flushed with indignation on both sides of the face. Was this possible? Was it a trick of the light from the setting sun? Perhaps the most logical explanation is that it was blood from the executioner's hands that stained her face. Le Gros was summoned to appear before the authorities and admonished for his actions as well as receiving a short prison sentence.

M.G. Duval, accompanied by a neighbour, witnessed the execution of Charlotte Corday. They had been standing close to the entrance to the Champs-Elysées and quite close to the scaffold, according to Duval's account, but they did not witness le Gros's outrageous insult to the dead woman. How close were they to the guillotine? The scaffold was originally placed between the statue of Louis XV and the entrance to the Champs-Elysées for the execution of the king in January the same year. By May 1793 it had been moved to a location between the Pedestal and the garden of the Tuileries. If M. Duval was standing near the Champs-Elysées, as he stated, then he would have been more distant from the scene than he thought. M. Duval also added that it was several days later that the rumour of the incident began to circulate in Paris.

On 9 June 1864 the guillotine had been assembled at the Place de la Roquette for the execution of Guy Couty de la Pommerais. A doctor by profession, Pommerais had been condemned to death after being found guilty of the double poisoning of his wife and mother-in-law. He was duly guillotined by Heindreicht the executioner.

Some seventy years before, in the days of the Revolution, Dr Jean-Joseph Sue, librarian at the Paris School of Medicine and the father of Eugène Sue the writer, became concerned over the dilemma that the guillotine posed. Did a severed head retain the faculty to think and also feel pain? He declared that it could indeed see, hear, smell, think and therefore conjecture upon its new state. Sue concluded that his theory could be proved if it was possible to arrange with the condemned man a code of movements or signs that could be identified after decapitation. He was convinced that consciousness could persist after the blade had fallen. The nineteenth-century author Villiers de l'Isle-Adam may have been prompted by Dr Sue's conclusions to write his story, *The Secret of the Scaffold*. It concerned an arrangement that was made between the condemned man Guy Couty de la Pommerais and Dr Velpeau, who frequently attended executions carried out at la Roquette. The story was widely accepted as fact and was even quoted as an example in the 1950s.

Both doctors, Velpeau the observer and Pommerais the condemned, came to an arrangement prior to the execution. Velpeau said to Pommerais: 'When the blade falls, I shall be standing opposite you, near to the machine. As speedily as possible, your head will be handed to me by the executioner, then I shall shout loudly in your ear; "M. Couty de la Pommerais, lower your right eye three times keeping your other eye open!"' Pommerais agreed to the arrangement. The story concluded as follows:

> The bloody head of Pommerais quivered in the hands of the surgeon, staining his fingers, cuffs and clothing. Velpeau shouted the pre-arranged question into the right ear; the result made him tremble with icy terror. The right eyelid of Pommerais lowered, the left eye opened wide staring at Velpeau. 'In the name of God and our being, repeat the sign twice!' shouted Velpeau. The eyes separated as if from an internal effort but the lid was not raised again. The face became rigid and emotionless.

Villiers de l'Isle-Adam had used real people in his story, which is probably why fact and fiction have been confused. Yes, Pommerais was guillotined. Yes, Dr Velpeau frequently attended executions in his professional capacity, though by chance on this occasion he was not present at la Roquette. The prison chaplain, Abbé Crozes, who was present, later gave his assurance that no test or experiment was ever carried out on the head of Couty de la Pommerais. This important experiment, then, was but a myth and merely a disturbing story.

Villiers de l'Isle-Adam was not opposed to the death penalty and thus had no ulterior motive in writing the story. A rather sadistic man, he was in fact a great supporter of the red device and deplored the attacks made upon it. He wished to retain the scaffold and its high steps, the great platform upon which the guillotine was mounted. He also disliked the watering-down of the drama when the machine was reduced to street level, where it appeared to be much less terrifying. When the story was written in 1883, some twenty years after Pommerais's execution, there was a new vitality behind the movement to abolish the death penalty, especially using the guillotine. Once again the debate was concerned with the ethics of using a device considered by some as a gruesome form of pre- and post-death torture. The call for it to be abandoned received little support. The guillotine and its adherents would triumph and the machine would continue to be used.

From the earliest days of the guillotine the question as to whether life could linger in a decapitated head had been of major concern to people. Charles-Henri Sanson was recorded as stating that when opposing members of the National Assembly were guillotined (presumably during the Thermidor cleansing), heads put into the same sack bit each other and proved difficult to separate! Other gruesome examples were given, such as headless corpses staggering across the scaffold, still maintaining the body's motor instincts. Such statements do not ring true, particularly those associated with Sanson. He and his sons were responsible for the execution of three thousand people during the Revolution, an achievement only surpassed in Nazi Germany, where a redesigned guillotine was used to remove Adolf Hitler's political opponents. Sanson, who knew everything, divulged nothing. He kept no authenticated diaries, and left no notes or memoirs. He carried out his task efficiently and silently, so such rambling tales and attributed quotations can only be construed as innuendo.

* * *

The concept of the survival of perception in a severed head was first actively considered by Dr Pierre Gautier in 1767, who at that time was a student of surgery in the Paris hospital of the Charité. Prior to 1793 decapitation was effected by the use of a sword, and was a rather haphazard affair. Such executions were rare as most felons were hanged or subjected to an array of other forms of capital punishment. After the introduction of the guillotine the subject of decapitation was to receive fresh attention. An important contribution to the debate came from Samuel Soemmering, a German doctor living in France. His views, as written to a colleague and pupil named Oestler, were published in the November 1795 issue of the paper *Le Moniteur*, by which time the guillotine was up and running. The letter to Oestler had originally been penned two years earlier in May 1793, four months after the execution of the king. It is not clear whether the letter was intended for publication or whether Oestler decided to submit it to the newspaper as a contentious statement concerning the new implement. In his letter Dr Soemmering authoritatively stated that sensation was *not* destroyed by the guillotine and concurred with the ideas expressed by Gautier twenty-five years earlier. His letter read:

> The seat of feeling and its perception lies within the brain. The workings of this consciousness of feeling can continue whether the circulation of blood within the brain be suspended, feeble or partial. The guillotine must be a horrible form of death! Feeling, personality and ego remain alive for some time within the head separated from the victim's body. There remains the conscious awareness of pain. If air could circulate through the vocal organs, the head would speak.

Dr Soemmering condemned the guillotine as a frightful piece of barbaric equipment that reduced a civilised society to the level of savages. Strong condemnation indeed, and in accord with doctors Gautier and Sue, but this was early days. Dr Soemmering would soon wish that he had been a little more discreet in his analysis as the big guns of the medical profession lined up against him. Nevertheless the effect of such damning censure must have been to create a living nightmare in the minds of those whose families and friends had perished beneath the guillotine's blade. Had their deaths been slow and agonising instead of instant and painless?

The pro-guillotine members of the medical profession prepared themselves for a vehement rebuttal of Soemmering's theories. To destroy his credibility, part of his own theory was turned against him. Quoting from one of Soemmering's earlier papers, Dr Sedillot stated: 'The faculty of perception or the consciousness of feelings ceases in ordinary sleep!' Dr Sedillot therefore argued that if the awareness of feelings ceased in ordinary sleep, how could it possibly be imagined that in death – following a punishment which obliterates all vital functions at a stroke – the awareness of feeling and pain could remain?

Dr Guillotin and his professional associates also refuted all such theories concerning life in the severed head. *Le Moniteur*'s pages were filled with strong arguments from the medical profession, castigating the opinions of Gautier, Sue and Soemmering. Numerous people spoke up for the guillotine and its humanitarian attributes, including many authoritative doctors and surgeons such as George Wedekind, le Pelletier, J.B. Leveille, Gastelier, Cabanis and of course Dr Sedillot. All were concerned about the doubts being raised over the efficacy of their virtuous guillotine. All concurred that death was without doubt instantaneous and that the guillotined suffered no after-pain or sense-perception. The onslaught from the medical profession seems to have had the desired effect on Dr Soemmering, who tactfully withdrew from the arena. Such powerful and authoritative medical opinions should have reassured the unenlightened and the ignorant, yet still the question hovered in the minds of many people and continued to haunt those who remained unconvinced. The imponderable question 'dead or alive?' would continue to be asked.

Soemmering may have been unaware of the research being carried out at the time of the Revolution; it was after all a perplexing problem and his own observations had been written some two years before being reported in *Le Moniteur*. Dr Seguret, a professor of anatomy, had been carrying out experiments on severed heads and his conclusions were in line with Soemmering's theories. The tests carried out by Seguret took place under laboratory conditions and the assessment of the results, if generally known, might have been very disturbing. Two heads were exposed to bright sunlight. The professor then opened the eyelids on each head, which resulted in the eyes closing immediately with 'an aliveness that was abrupt and startling. The face assumed an expression of intense suffering. The protruding tongue on one of the heads was pricked by an assistant using a scalpel. The tongue withdrew into the mouth and the facial features grimaced as if in pain.' In a third trial the head of an assassin named Terrier was subjected to similar tests; it was found that fifteen minutes after the time of decapitation the eyes continued to focus in the direction of the man who was speaking.

Such controversial test results, if true and accurate, would probably have been subject to a strong degree of censorship or simply kept secret. At this point more than half of the medical profession had denigrated Soemmering's theories as being ridiculous and it would need a brave man to state otherwise and run counter to mainstream medical opinion.

It was of paramount importance at a time of mass executions not to destroy the public's confidence in the guillotine or to lay the foundation of doubt over the 'dead or alive' issue. The guillotine was an instrument of justice, and its adoption as a humanitarian method to legally take away a life could not be impugned. After all, reputations were also at stake. Nevertheless the idea would not go away.

Doubts still persisted, reinforcing the absent Dr Soemmering's theories. Had not Haller stated that the head of a guillotined man grimaced horribly when a surgeon present at the execution inserted a finger into his rachidian canal? Did not Weikard see the lips of a decapitated man move as if trying to speak? Had not Leveling insisted that, while present on the execution square, he had (in the interests of science) personally irritated part of the spinal marrow which had remained attached to the head after decapitation? The convulsion of the head, he stated, was appalling.

Such claims may have been later denied as circumstantial or hearsay, but they did nothing to inspire confidence in the minds of others. Were such outrageous statements the product of imaginary forces, hysteria or paranoia? The contemporary understanding of the human mind was limited, and the problem itself one which would have perplexed philosophers, theologians and lawyers, not just doctors. If only the head could speak and describe, if any, its feelings. The whole concept must be preposterous, but . . .

In 1804 Georges Cadoudal and his fellow conspirators were condemned to the guillotine. Twenty-six men would perish beneath the blade for plotting against Napoleon I. On this occasion the efficiency of the guillotine and the executioner's skill were unsurpassed. Henri Sanson would take only twenty-seven minutes to complete the executions, a dispatch rate of almost one every minute. By chance the severed head of one of the victims, Coster de Saint Victor, flew from the torso with considerable velocity. The head fell from the scaffold and rolled down on to the cobbled square. An assistant quickly retrieved it and tossed it into one of the open baskets used for disposing of the bodies. Some of those present at the scene insisted that Coster's decapitated head had actually uttered a few words! The authorities denied this revelation as totally preposterous.

As time passed, execution on a grand scale, like that of the Cadoudal conspirators, became less frequent, diminishing the chances of observing moving heads or bodies. The interest in the 'dead or alive' issue waned until 1836, when the execution took place of the murderer Pierre François Lacenaire. He believed that he would maintain his vital senses after being guillotined and may have prompted Dr Lelut of Bicêtre to test the theory. Dr Lelut also wanted to find out if consciousness persisted after decapitation. Lacenaire agreed that after his execution he would attempt to close his left eye and leave the right eye open. After he had been guillotined, his head was removed and carefully observed for a considerable time. Dr Lelut was unable to detect any form of conscious awareness in the features of the late Lacenaire. The test was a complete failure, or perhaps, depending upon one's point of view, a complete success! Lelut merely observed the head and did not attempt to prompt any residual signs of life. The guillotine was exonerated with the instantaneous demise of Lacenaire.

It was not until 1879, ninety years after Dr Soemmering's critical attack upon the machine, that any real scientific interest was aroused and produced documented experimentation. An attempt would be made to prove if life was retained for a short time after guillotining. The awakened interest in the subject soon found for doctors E. Decaisne, G. Decaisne and Evrard an ideal candidate for their test.

The murderer Theotime Prunier was to be guillotined on 13 November at 7am. Prunier was a 23-year-old murderer and a necrophiliac, his victim an elderly woman. Her corpse had been sexually violated before being thrown into the river. Some time later Prunier returned to the spot where he had disposed of the body, dragged it from the river and sexually violated it again. Arrested the following morning, he was eventually tried for murder and condemned to death. The guillotine was assembled outside Beauvais prison to await Prunier's arrival. The doctors doubtless regarded him as an admirable specimen for the experiment. He was a strongly built man of brutish appearance. On the morning of the execution his pulse rate was checked and found to have increased to eighty-four per minute, though outwardly he seemed calm and resigned. Five minutes had elapsed since his execution when the doctors received the separated head and body. The face was pale, dull and there were no bloodstains around the lips and ears, indicating the absence of convulsive movements following beheading. They recorded: 'The eyes were closed. If one half-opened the lids, the eyeballs were seen to be fixed and sunken. The pupils were equal in size and somewhat dilated. The face, completely bloodless, wore a look of astonishment.'

The next part of their experiment took place in the cemetery grounds. They called Prunier's name loudly and repeatedly, but it caused no responsive movement in the eyes or in the face that might have suggested awareness. The doctors next pinched the cheek firmly, then inserted into the nostrils a brush saturated in concentrated ammonia. A lighted candle was next held close to the eyes and silver nitrate drawn across the eye surface. The results indicated no movement or the slightest contraction.

The test results may have been a big disappointment for the

doctors, but for those with faith in the Timbers of Justice they spelled out a total success. Perception in a severed head cannot be proved! But one important fact remains to be considered. Approximately thirty minutes had elapsed between Prunier being guillotined and the completion of the tests carried out by the anatomists. What might have occurred in the lapse of time was worthy of further debate.

A year later it was the turn of Louis Ménesclou, a child rapist and murderer, to face the guillotine. An experiment carried out upon his severed head by Dr Dassy de Lignières was, to say the least, somewhat unethical. This experiment involved the attempted regeneration of the head, rather than simple observation. There was a time lapse of up to three hours before the tests were finished. On 7 September 1880 the doctor began to pump blood from a living dog into Ménesclou's severed head. The result of this unorthodox transfusion was startling and grotesque. As the blood circulated through the head, the face reddened, the lips swelled and coloured visibly and the features sharpened in intensity. Dr de Lignières reported excitedly: 'This is no longer the livid and flaccid mask of a minute before. This head is about to speak for it has just become animated by the beating of a heart.'

Grim conclusions were already being drawn concerning the guillotine, as the Frankenstein-like experiment continued. For a period of two seconds Ménesclou's lips began to stammer silently, the eyelids twitched and the whole face seemed to have been awakened into a state of amazement and shock. Dr Lignières was now fully convinced of the validity of his tests. 'There is no worse torture than decapitation with the machine invented by that sensitive and humanitarian deputy Dr Guillotin . . . when the head has rolled into the sawdust, this head separated from its body hears the voices of the crowd, the decapitated victim feels himself dying in the basket. He sees the guillotine and the light of day,' he reported.

Ménesclou's head soon returned to a state of rigor mortis but without the benefit to science of uttering one single word! The dog was unharmed, and suffered no ill-effects from its unique experience. Dr de Lignières advised that the executioners should immediately shake the decapitated head in the air to ensure that any residual blood flowed from the brain and therefore reduced the chance of further or prolonged suffering to the victim.

The experiment may have had some merit in attempting to answer an intractable issue, but it should also be asked whether or not Ménesclou's severed head could retain its faculties without the sustenance of a donor's blood. The law was precise and clearly stated that no form of torture should be inflicted upon the condemned, but no one seems to have foreseen that one day someone would want to ask if the definition of torture included actions carried out on a corpse in the pursuit of research.

In 1905, twenty-five years after the Ménesclou experiment, a series of remarkable events concerning the murderer Languille took place. His execution was carried out on the morning of 28 June at 5.30am, just before daybreak. Dr Beaurieux carried out observational tests on the severed head of the victim by loudly calling his name. There was no time-lapse between the execution and the doctor's observations, which began immediately after the head fell. The authenticity of the doctor's report is in no doubt and it did much to confirm the idea that perception and consciousness could persist in a decapitated head at least for a number of seconds. In Dr Beaurieux's own words, now lodged in the criminal archives, the remarkable events of the day unfolded thus:

It is necessary to understand that the criminal Languille displayed extraordinary sang-froid and courage from the time he was informed that this was his last hour, to when he walked firmly to the guillotine. It may very well be that the circumstances for observation and consequently the resulting phenomena vary enormously according to whether the condemned retain their self-control or whether they are in such a state of physical and mental anxiety that they have to be carried to the place of execution and are already half dead as if paralysed by the anguish of the fatal moment that is to come.

Languille's head fell on the severed surface of the neck and therefore I did not have to lift it up in my hands. I was not obliged even to touch it in order to position it upright. Chance had served me well for the observation which I wished to make.

This is what I was able to observe immediately following decapitation: the eyelids and lips of the guillotined prisoner worked in irregular rhythmic contractions for five or six seconds. I waited for several seconds, the spasms then ceased, the face relaxed, the lids half closed on the eyeballs leaving only the white conjunctiva visible, exactly as in the dying whom we have occasion to see every day in the course of our profession.

It was then that I shouted in a strong sharp voice, 'Languille!' I then observed the eyelids slowly lift up without spasmodic contraction but with an even movement, quite distinct and normal as happens in everyday life with people awakened or torn from their thoughts. Languille's eyes definitely fixed themselves on mine and the pupils focused themselves. It was not a vague or dull look without expression that is observed on any day in dying people to whom one speaks. I saw undeniably living eyes which were looking back at me.

After several more seconds the eyelids closed again slowly and evenly and the head regained the same appearance as it had before I had called out. I called out the name again and once more without spasm the eyelids lifted and living eyes fixed themselves on mine with even more penetration than the first time, then there was a further closing of the eyelids, but now less complete.

I called 'Languille!' a third time. There was no further movement, and the eyes took on a glazed look as in the dead. The whole thing had lasted twenty-five to thirty seconds.

Dr Beaurieux also added that a colleague, Dr Pettigand, who witnessed an execution in which the head likewise fell upon the severed section of the neck, thereby reducing haemorrhage to a minimum, saw the eyes of the decapitated man fix themselves on his and follow him round in a circular motion. The eyes of the severed head even pursued Pettigand when he changed direction in an effort to escape from its gaze.

The echoes of Soemmering's theories one hundred years before can be heard in the opinion formed by Dr Beaurieux. A superior reflex can occur and the brain retains survival of all its elements. In the case of Languille, the sense of hearing and the sense of sight were retained and survived for twenty-five seconds after the blade of the guillotine had fallen. Drawing further conclusions, Beaurieux argued that if the survival of the lower brain is admitted, then why not the survival of the upper brain too? The cortex may similarly survive, leaving open the possibility of conscious perception. Such reality, however, can only be revealed by the subject of the experiment, which again shows the problem as an insoluble one, but worthy of further discussion.

Throughout the history of the guillotine the medical controversy concerning the 'dead or alive' issue continued to be a contentious subject. The consensus of opinion based upon international research suggested that of all forms of capital punishment, the guillotine was believed to have been the least painful and therefore the most merciful. Research on comparative forms of execution was carried out in France, England and Germany. All these countries, either in their medieval history or in their immediate past, had used a pseudo-guillotine.

What of the opinion of the executioners themselves and the professional technicians who maintained the guillotine? They supervised or took part in many hundreds of executions during their long careers. Georges Martin, an assistant executioner, attended at 120 executions during the 1930s and 1940s. He retired in 1947 after twenty years service to the republic. Of this number, he was able to observe carefully some sixty individual cases. In his professional opinion no cerebral survival remained immediately after execution and the loss of life, including perception of the senses, was instant. Between the fall of the blade and his examination of the decapitated head, the time elapsed was only three or four seconds. His observations in all cases remained the same, irrespective of the state of anxiety displayed by the individual criminals prior to their guillotining.

After an execution, Georges recorded:

The eyes were fixed, dilated, almost out of their sockets. The immobility of the eyelids was total. The eyes very soon became glassy. The lips were already white and presented a particular aspect, like a piece of silk paper or like the surface of a deflated red balloon. The face appeared waxen.

My observations led to the conclusion that cerebral survival was not possible. However, it often happens that the body continues to move after the head is separated. I observed this phenomenon twice.

He went on to describe two individual cases.

The execution at Perigueux of Firmin Cipierre, 29 July 1930, an individual with marked criminal traits – the epitome of the classic murderer, a brute of a man with receding forehead and an almost complete lack of frontal lobes. A man of arrested development, almost a moron. He was a man of powerful musculature but with very small feet and hands which caused difficulty when tying his bonds.

On the morning of the execution, the condemned man was extremely agitated, the wardens had made a mistake. When he had asked for a glass of rum, thinking that they were doing him a favour he was allowed to drink the whole of the contents and they eventually brought him to us [the executioners] in a state of wild excitement. The second mistake was that they had also removed his handcuffs before handing him over to us. Whilst in the office, Cipierre saw the prosecutor who had asked for the death sentence and rushed at him. We attempted to overpower him but it was not easy. The tables, chairs and files were thrown all over the room. Deibler [the chief executioner] received a blow from the man's fist which pushed his bowler hat down over his eyes. Finally Obrecht [an assistant executioner] brought Cipierre down and we managed to bind him. Anatole Deibler cut short the 'toilette'. The condemned man, still furious, was propelled on to the guillotine whilst still at the height of his excitement.

When the blade had fallen, the head took on the aspect that I have already described. Death was instantaneous, but the body continued to writhe. The arms were dragging at the ropes and this horrible phenomenon lasted for some minutes. Even twenty minutes later at the cemetery, the body was still trembling.

The execution of Marcel Garnotal, guillotined with the Nazi spy Fritz Erler on 6 June 1940. Garnotal had been found guilty of a sadistic crime at Aulnay-sous-Bois. He was a congenital abnormal who ought to have been confined long before his crime. This time I noticed very clear-cut reactions on the part of the body. The observation was cut short because an air raid warning forced us to hurry. The head never shows any survival but the body occasionally does There is no survival of consciousness but only a non coordinated nervous agitation.

As the turmoil over the ethics of capital punishment continued, so did the experiments. The most damning remarks of all were made in a report completed by two instructors of forensic medicine, Professors R. Piedelièvre and Etienne Fournier. Their report was submitted to the Academy of Medicine in 1953, but was not published until three years later. Their conclusions are expressed so strongly that the main passage of the article is quoted here in full.

For a number of years the removal of organs has been permitted by law after the punishment of death. If we are allowed to express our opinion on this subject, such sights are astonishingly painful. The blood flows from the vessels to the rhythm of the severed carotids before coagulating. The muscles contract and their fibrillation is amazing. The intestine wriggles and the heart undergoes irregular, incomplete and fascinating movements. The mouth sometimes contracts into an appalling grimace. It is true that in the decapitated head the eyes are motionless with the pupils dilated. Fortunately they cannot see and although they are glassy with no corpse-like opalescence they do not move; their transparency is vivid but their fixity is mortal. All this can last for minutes and even for hours in healthy subjects; death is not immediate.

In our anxiety we have often thought of these poor human remains, which were once part of a whole to which we belong, buried after the execution, living partially in their tombs, without thought admittedly, for we know that the loss of consciousness is swift, the brain not being irrigated and without oxygen, ceasing its capability of thought within a few seconds.

In another term of reference we also know that each coagulation of the blood is a vital phenomenon which ceases after death. This is why in the course of a post mortem, attention has to be paid to bruises. They are proof that a lesion – possibly traumatic – took place during life. But if the blood arrested in the wounds inflicted upon a corpse does not congeal, it means that death, in its normal definition of being the cessation of breathing and circulation, has taken place some time before. The following example is characteristic: we recently undertook the post mortem of a subject whose spinal marrow had been removed six hours after death. The forensic examination carried out the next day showed the presence of congealed blood in the region of the cuts. At first sight one might have said that the first intervention had been carried out on a living person.

Doctors Piedelièvre and Fournier, having examined a number of guillotined corpses, concluded with a fearful and awe-inspiring declaration: 'Every vital element survives decapitation. The doctor is left with the impression of a horrible experience, of a murderous vivisection followed by a premature burial.'

Dead or Alive?

It is reasonable to assume that both doctors were present at a number of executions and their observations indicate that sense-perception can remain for an unspecified time. Their reports of body contractions immediately following guillotining support the statements of Georges Martin, but most frightening of all is the statement referring to a corpse in which blood can still congeal post mortem!

In 1981 the guillotine was finally abandoned. Instead of an instrument of justice it became an historical artefact, a museum piece resurrected only for the purpose of theatre and cinema spectacles. Years of scientific enquiries into the question of 'dead or alive?' have not apparently provided a definitive answer. There have been experts who accepted it and those who rejected it. Modern-day physiologists invited to offer an insight into such theories generally decline to comment on the grotesque possibility that a decapitated head sliced off so quickly by the guillotine could still be aware of events in the outer – and inner – world.

9

The Guillotine and the Executioners

Since the invention of the guillotine, my father and I merely supervise – everything is done by our assistants,' said Henri Sanson, son of the great Charles-Henri Sanson. The role of executioner may be socially sanctioned, depending on particular circumstances, but it has rarely been socially welcomed. In France, people who accepted the concept of capital punishment none the less shunned the man who carried it out. It is hard to understand how a human being can come to terms with the – admittedly legal – employment of putting to death members of his own species. The executioner remains apart, a different kind of killer; clearly he is not a lawless murderer, nor is he a soldier, whose primary role is the defence of his nation. The executioner is involved in the process of judicial retribution. Though at times of high emotion people often express a willingness to 'do the deed', it is unlikely that many would actually have the nerve to go through with it. So what kind of men were they, the executioners, and what kind of interest did the public, whose servants they were, take in their grisly craft?

During the years of the Revolution men pleaded to be recruited as assistant executioners; it was considered an honourable vocation, helping to cleanse the new Republic of its enemies. The chief executioner had considerable status, and, though feared, was also respected. In those uncertain times the scaffold became the stage where the drama of life and death was played out on a grand scale, and where the executioner always had the leading role. The courage and composure of the guillotine's victims encouraged the mob to regard the executions as entertainment, carefully cultivated pantomimes of indifference and death, skilfully directed by the executioner himself. Had more people been dragged to their deaths screaming in terror and begging for mercy, like the unfortunate Madame du Barry, perhaps the mob would have been repelled instead of thrilled, and public opinion might have changed towards the Timbers of Justice. But as it was, the thunderous guillotine and its headsman became the focal point of revolutionary life, death and excitement.

Such was the impact of the red machine that it was also reproduced in miniature. Children played with toy guillotines, sometimes decapitating small rodents and birds. Especially popular with women were small silver or gold earrings in the shape of the guillotine, and in some of the salons or clubs, including those of the Girondins, miniature working-model guillotines served as table decorations. When the dessert was served, tiny mannequins made to resemble infamous republicans such as Danton, Robespierre or Tinville were guillotined. As the head was severed, a crimson liquid flowed from the doll's neck, into which ladies would dip their handkerchiefs. The mannequin was actually a disguised perfume vial and the ichor its scented contents. The guillotine had become an icon and was never far from the centre of attention. Guillotineomania was a reality.

The machine was always of timber construction. Attempts to modernise it failed, largely because the executioner, who was also the keeper of the device, tended to be uncooperative and resistant to change. Successive headsmen knew their machine well and had confidence in its performance just the way it was. It had once been proposed to make it entirely in metal and to mount it upon wheels to make it more portable. M. Heindreicht, the executioner appointed chief in 1849, objected to the idea, finally dismissing it as impracticable. The guillotine, as Heindreicht explained, was a precision instrument and after assembly had to stand absolutely vertical to guarantee its efficient operation, while the surface upon which it stood needed to be perfectly horizontal.

Guillotine

It may well be that Heindreicht had in mind the execution of the poet and assassin Pierre François Lacenaire on 9 January 1836. He and his accomplice Pierre Avril were both guillotined by Clément-Henri Sanson, but the execution was not without incident. The self-styled poet and anti-hero was obsessed and haunted by the guillotine. He had always believed that someday his life would end beneath its great blade. Even his calling cards were inscribed with the words 'fiancé of the guillotine' after his name. Found guilty of an attempt to kill Louis Philippe, and of the murder of the widow Chardon and her son, Lacenaire would soon keep his appointment with the guillotine. Somewhat masochistically, the popular poet even recorded in words what he thought would be the post-experience of his own execution. The bard of the condemned cell was undoubtedly psychotic, and yet to many of his admirers he remained a hero.

The guillotine had been erected at the Place Saint-Jacques. A crowd of more than five hundred had gathered on a freezing morning to witness Lacenaire's farewell performance. Members of the Municipal Guard were in attendance to keep control of the agitated crowd. Avril was guillotined first, without incident. Then Lacenaire was strapped tightly upon the *bascule* and pushed into the arms of his nightmare bride. As the blade thundered down, it came to an abrupt halt just above Lacenaire's neck. The *mouton* had somehow become jammed in the grooves of the uprights (Sanson wrote that the machine was perhaps tired, not having had to perform two executions one after the other for a long time!). The heavy knife was hauled back up to its full height and released again. But its fall was again interrupted, the blade slamming to a halt just inches away from the victim's neck. What should have been over in less than a second now ran on into its fourth minute. A nervous executioner hauled the blade aloft again and released it for a third time. Lacenaire, still immobilised in the *lunette*, somehow managed to turn his head far enough to look upwards as the blade made its final and successful descent. It was a look, according to the executioner, that had more of surprise than fear in it.

The Guillotine and the Executioners

The newspaper reporters who witnessed the fiasco did not spare the executioner and concentrated upon the needless suffering of the victim. They refused to print an official statement that the event had been accomplished without incident. The awful performance was vilified in the popular press and Lacenaire was transformed into an heroic figure in death.

Successive chief executioners were required to be virtuosos of their instrument, performing before a critical public. They had to be highly skilled in the technique of their unsavoury but unique craft. Their efficiency and the deployment of their assistants in dispatching some unfortunate wretch would be widely commented upon. People wanted to see a particular kind of decorum joined to a virtuoso display of kinetics in bringing off a polished performance – given this, good press reviews were inevitable. The news reporters and curious onlookers that gathered about the scaffold were always in an expectant mood. Would the victim struggle or would he display unexpected courage? Would the execution be without incident, and would it be accomplished in a new record time? The guillotine never lost its power to thrill and entertain.

Despite the popularity of the guillotine and the general public's support for capital punishment, the executioner was viewed somewhat differently. In Paris, the cultural capital of the world, the executioner's vocation was subject to ancient prejudices that were never wholly dispelled. Some executioners were viewed as more efficient than others, and some were actually admired, but the general attitude to their post in society was one of disdain. The appointee, his wife and family could seldom escape the prejudice levelled against them and found little acceptance outside their own sphere. Their social world generally revolved around their own kind – other executioners. Interestingly, the public's prejudice against executioners lasted throughout the history of the guillotine, although it was seldom levelled at the machine itself.

Across the English Channel things were very different. What would a Deibler or Desfourneaux not have given to be as esteemed and appreciated as their English counterparts!

Albert Pierrepoint, for example, was hugely popular in England – people clamoured to shake his hand or ask for his autograph or buy him a drink. Perhaps it was the fearsome guillotine itself that was responsible for the ignominy and contempt in which the executioners were held. Its operators and technicians were not the masters of the machine, but its servants. Their bloodstained hands made them outcasts. Even the self-serving politician was more popular than the poor *bourreau*. It was only in the period between 1900 and 1910 that the fickle public, which still adored the guillotine, suddenly accelerated the executioner's popularity and set aside the traditional prejudices. The old and pernicious attitude changed radically as the *bourreau*, albeit only temporarily, attained almost cult status.

Armand Fallières, who was President of France in 1907, was a firm opponent of capital punishment, but was unable to persuade his peers to change the law. Over the years the moderates had gained several victories in their attempts to outlaw the guillotine, or at least to remove it from public view and put an end to public executions. In fact public executions would continue for another half century, finally coming to an end in 1939, but in 1898 the National Assembly had approved a motion that took the first step along that road. Henceforth all executions within the capital would take place at a single location, in front of the prison wall of La Santé on the Boulevard Arago. Doubtless some people hoped that this decision would curtail the numbers of onlookers. Such views were partially influenced by the huge crowds that had gathered for the executions of Allorto and Sellier, allegedly compromising public safety in the process.

Although President Fallières failed in his attempts to do away with the guillotine, he took advantage of his position and commuted all death sentences to terms of imprisonment. He was able to do so because all final appeals against the sentence were reviewed by the incumbent president, who then had the right to make the final decision. This power effectively gave Fallières a veto over the judicial process.

The Guillotine and the Executioners

Many years later, in 1969, the newly elected president Georges Pompidou also promised that no executions would occur while he remained in office, and in a show of good faith he commuted four death sentences. However, like Armand Fallières before him, Pompidou could no more control his own destiny than any other man. An elected politician who insists upon strict adherence to his own unbending viewpoint at the expense of the wider perspective soon has to retract. His views were not supported by the nation at large – and when the nation speaks even presidents must listen.

Fallières had effectively shunned the guillotine. Keeping faith with his beliefs, he continued to commute all death sentences forwarded to him. Anatole Deibler, the chief executioner, was now seemingly redundant but was hailed by a disgruntled populace as a public defender. Influential newspapers and periodicals began to bestow upon their executioner the status of a cult hero, maintaining for him a high profile through the guillotine's lean years. As Fallières commuted yet another death sentence, the shout could be heard, 'Long live Deibler!'

But then Fallières made a serious error of judgement. Again he used his presidential powers to commute the death sentence of a hated and despised child murderer named Solleilland. The already restless Parisians were outraged; their cry now became 'Long live the guillotine!' They refused to sit idly by and allow such appalling crimes to be apparently set aside. The political ramifications were wide-ranging. The backlash of public fury ensured that execution was once again the penalty for serious crimes, rather than imprisonment or banishment to French Guiana. M. Deibler, a third-generation executioner, and his two guillotines would soon be back in business again. Oddly enough, as soon as the blade began to fall, so also did the executioner's popularity. The fickle public saw in the executioner only a necessary evil and the old prejudices again began to surface.

For the executioner, it was a confusing situation: the same set of values resulted in acclamation for judges and juries and contempt for the executioner. If the jury at a murder trial refused to recommend clemency for a guilty man, they would be publicly commended for maintaining their principles. No one would lose sleep over the outcome of their deliberations, yet they were only one step away from being executioners themselves. It was inconceivable that the public prosecutor could demand the death sentence, and a Tribunal Judge could impose it, and yet they remained on their high pedestals as defenders of right and justice. It was inconceivable that the President of the Republic, who had the authority to commute a death sentence but did not do so for political reasons, could rise to the highest pinnacle of popularity, his argument being that there should be no interference in the judicial process of law. The same kind of hypocrisy permitted the public to be outraged by the actions of a murderer, while society condoned and even welcomed capital punishment. Was it not all of society that tacitly executed the criminal? But of all the people involved in the whole spectrum of crime and punishment, it was only the lineage executioner, after a thousand years of service to society, that was despised. It seemed there was justice for everyone except the headsman.

Prior to 1847, and the ignominious discharge of Clément-Henri Sanson, the guillotine was the property of the executioner and not the state. Condemned felons were contracted out to him for the sentence to be carried out. As soon as the condemned person's appeal for clemency was rejected by the President of the Republic, they effectively became the property of the executioner, who then carried out the demands of the law. Successive executioners bore the responsibility for the machine's upkeep and safe storage. In 1871 the roles of guillotine and executioner were reversed and the machine itself was 'executed'. It was during the Commune that the 137th Battalion of the Eleventh Quarter, where the guillotine was then kept, appropriated the machine from the executioner. It was smashed and burned before an exuberant crowd assembled at the foot of the statue of Voltaire. It was to be the people's revenge upon a device that had cut off so many of their comrades' heads. However, with the restoration of order also came the restoration of the guillotine.

The Guillotine and the Executioners

The main aim of the executioner was to care for and, if possible, perfect his machine. His nightmares were not about death but about the awful possibility of the guillotine malfunctioning. The worst possible scenario was a blade jamming when the head was only partially severed, in front of a critical and damning audience. No executioner wanted a repeat of Lacenaire's demise. Small refinements and improvements were often made to the guillotine to improve its performance and thus creditably reflect upon its servants. Henri Sanson, who was the chief executioner for forty-six years, altered the method of attaching the blade to the *mouton*, its heavy weight. The numerous bolts and metal collars were replaced by just three large, heavy-duty bolts. Active as an assistant executioner during the Revolution, he officiated, with his father, at the greatest number of executions in the history of the French guillotine. He was officially employed from 1795 until 1841, when he was succeeded by his son, the disreputable Clément-Henri. Dismissed from his post in 1847 after only six years of head-slicing, Clément-Henri brought to an end the long reign of the Sansons.

Charles André Férey succeeded Sanson in 1847. But it was Heindreicht that was responsible for making some subtle alterations to the apparatus of execution. Aware of the humanitarian concerns that had brought about the machine's creation, Heindreicht attempted to make the whole issue of head-lopping far more user-friendly. On 25 November 1870 he accepted the views of the Minister of Justice Adolfe Crémieux, and duly abolished the high platform and steps that had supported the red machine. Reduced to ground level and its stage abandoned, the guillotine no longer offered the same opportunity for great dramas. No longer could the elevated platform allow the condemned to make their great theatrical and oratorical farewells. At ground level the guillotine seemed much less terrifying and awe-inspiring. Heindreicht also painted the glittering steel blade a discreet and mournful black. No more would its highly polished surface reflect the dancing rays of the early morning sun to dazzle the eyes. Indeed, he became so sympathetic to the victims' plight that he further disguised the machine's appearance by painting its blood-red arms in a more soothing and less fearsome dark brown. Heindreicht was appointed the first National Executioner for all of France and Algeria by the decree of 1870, and he and his five aides swept away the old and garish ways, stamping his own mark of authority on the newly refurbished guillotine.

During 1869 all of France was shocked to learn of a particularly brutal murder. Jean-Baptiste Troppmann, just twenty-one years old, had violently murdered a family of eight. The appalling crime was avidly reported by the press and remained priority news for months. Showing no remorse, the young mass-murderer was found guilty and sentenced to be guillotined. The execution date, kept secret from Troppmann, was eventually arranged for daybreak on 19 January. The scantily bearded youth had become the most recognisable figure in Paris. Portraits of him adorned every stationery shop and kiosk throughout the whole of the city. The public's disgust at the motiveless slaughter of a mother and her children ensured that the execution would become an event to remember. Here at last was someone who really deserved to feel the guillotine's blade on the back of his neck . . . As for the executioner, well, his popularity was undoubtedly on the ascendant. Heindreicht, tall, grey-haired and handsome, was reported to have been treated with a complimentary and respectful familiarity, as befitted an executioner carrying out society's wishes.

Twenty-four hours before the sinister drama began to unfold, crowds of interested onlookers began assembling at the Place de la Roquette. Like eager cinema-goers at a premiere, they also congregated early enough to catch a glimpse of the special guests who had been given a privileged invitation for the execution. They included Maxime du Camp, a leading authority on social life and the world of the elite in the capital. He was accompanied by the distinguished Russian author Ivan Turgenev, who, on entering the prison, had been mistaken for the executioner. Another guest was the famous playwright

The Guillotine and the Executioners

Victorien Sardou, author of several of the plays in which Sarah Bernhardt achieved her greatest successes. The atmosphere was one of a celebrated social event.

In an attempt to maintain control over the proceedings, a large contingent of gendarmes and military personnel had assembled outside the prison, keeping a watchful eye on the crowds. The prison governor's guests were ushered to the second floor of the prison and in his comfortable quarters were served a buffet meal. The prison pharmacist also entered into the festivities and made time to entertain several of his own acquaintances to a frugal meal of truffled turkey. On such an occasion the guests, secure in the knowledge that after the Troppmann festivities they at least would adjourn to the comfort of their own homes, had no hesitation in agreeing that this was one of the governor's most successful and entertaining receptions. Outside the prison the mood was also one of cordiality, as the troops and gendarmes were served ample mugs of piping hot coffee. How fortunate it was that Troppmann, being such a villain, was unable to dampen the carnival atmosphere prevailing on that cold January morning. If indeed anyone had remembered to ask after him, they would have been informed that he was fast asleep and untroubled.

In the Place de la Roquette loud applause broke out as the elegant Heindreicht arrived with two black wagons and began carrying out the assembly of the machine. It was some time after midnight that the guillotine itself arrived and by 3am the gendarmes and guards were controlling a crowd numbering almost twenty thousand. Mounted police had arrived to assist in keeping order. By now the governor's guests had left their comfortable quarters to inspect at first sight the sinister apparatus that would shortly usher Troppmann into the next world. Caught up in the prevailing atmosphere of geniality, the executioner proudly explained the workings of the guillotine, pointing out the finer details of the mechanism to an enthralled audience. M. Sardou, extrovertly playful, insisted on being placed on to the weigh-plank, a little eccentricity that was applauded by his companions, who had drunk enough wine to exhibit a certain degree of joviality. The executioner entered into the spirit of the game; seizing hold of the comic playwright, he pushd him on to the *bascule*. Victorien Sardou closed his eyes. A bale of straw lay in the *lunette* where his head would have been if the *bascule* had been pushed forwards on its rollers. A loud click was heard and the elevated blade flashed down with a deep throaty roar, slicing through the straw bale not far from the head of the humorous playwright. The game had been exciting, a tantalising taste of what was to come. Everyone was in good humour and delighted with the efficiency of Heindreicht's machine. Of course, for Jean-Baptiste Troppmann, the approaching situation was much more sinister, but his would be perhaps the most important contribution to the unfolding melodrama.

As the time of the execution drew near, the prison officials, privileged guests and a priest arrived at the condemned man's cell. Refusing the traditional offer of a mug of Cognac, Troppmann was divested of the obligatory straitjacket and was given a clean white shirt to put on, which he carefully buttoned up with steady hands. Next he put on his shoes and walked resolutely out of his cell, watched by the curious celebrities. He remained silent and took little notice of the people around him. He was escorted to another room, where the only furnishings were a small stool and table. Troppmann sat down as Heindreicht and one of his aides entered to complete the ritual *toilette du condamné*. The executioner was smartly dressed in a black coat with white necktie, and looked more like a diplomat than a headsman. Two other assistants began to bind the condemned man's hands and feet. Heindreicht supervised the cutting of the victim's hair and the removal of the shirt collar. All the while Troppmann kept his head lowered like an obedient schoolboy until the preliminaries were completed. While the priest was still speaking, the executioner's aides took Troppmann out of the cell towards the door that led to the prison courtyard and beyond.

As the prison gates opened the excited noise of the immediate crowds burst in. Troppmann hobbled along half carried by Heindreicht's aides, his leg restraints interfering with and shortening his steps. In sixty more seconds it would be finished. Troppmann, temporarily separated from his escort, climbed the steps of the scaffold. The executioner was standing to the left of the guillotine, his hand near the lever that would release the blade. On the scaffold the victim stood for a moment, looking around, and suddenly two men seized him and speedily forced him onto the *bascule*. The crowd saw his feet kicking in the air, trying to regain his balance as the weigh-plank tilted downwards. Now thrust forward and into the uprights, his neck was encircled with the *lunette*. As if suddenly determined not to die like a sacrificial sheep, Troppmann made one last gesture of rebellion against authority. With extraordinary strength, he managed to arch his back and pull his head into the collar that encircled his neck. An assistant executioner made a grab for his hair and pulled him back into position. As the mighty blade fell with a hollow screeching sound, Troppmann made one last assault on the society that had condemned him. Stretching his neck forward as if to receive the strike of the blade, he sank his teeth deep into the assistant's hand, almost biting clean through the index finger. The assistant was the future chief executioner Nicolas Roch.

Despite various subtle attempts to demythologise the rituals surrounding public executions, by the end of the nineteenth century interest in seeing the guillotine in action was on the increase. Attempts by moderates to have capital punishment abandoned were not successful and public interest in watching an execution on the guillotine was never more graphically expressed than during the Paris Universal Exposition. Paris was awash with tourists enjoying everything that the City of Light could offer. In 1889, at the height of the Exposition, Jean-Baptiste Sellier and Joseph Allorto were both to be guillotined on the 17 August. The double execution proved to be the biggest crowd-puller of the Parisian festival, outdoing all the other spectacles. Thomas Cook & Co., the original travel agency, entered into the spirit of the occasion by laying on special chartered buses – it was, after all, the first execution in the city for three years. With the guillotine now at ground level, the scaffold having been abandoned during Heindreicht's tenure, there was very little to be seen without a special invitation. Barriers were erected around the guillotine in order to keep the spectators at a safe distance and yet the event was a sell-out. Every room in the houses surrounding the square had been hired out, and all the hotels and guest houses were fully booked. Every window was packed with eager faces, and some people even climbed up ladders to obtain a better view. Such was the magnetism of a double execution. Though the volume of the crowd guaranteed that most would actually see very little, simply being present at the execution seemed satisfying enough. Louis Deibler, the appointed National Executioner, guillotined Sellier and Allorto in just a few minutes. The excitement of the crowds lasted much longer and continued throughout the day.

When Heindreicht died in 1872 his death was announced by Léon Berger and Edourard Desfourneaux, both of whom came from executing families. The government appointed Nicolas Roch as his successor. His grandfather, one Antoine Roch, had been the executioner at Briey. In 1843 Nicolas had replaced the late François Desmorets as the executioner at Lons le Saulnier and ten years later succeeded Henri Ganier at Amiens. On attaining the title of Monsieur de Paris in 1872, his aides or assistants included a Ganier, a Desfourneaux and a Berger, all of whose families had been executioners in the days of the Revolution and before. In 1795 there had been 160 executioners in France. From the time of Heindreicht's appointment there would be only one, and now it was Nicolas Roch.

The executioners of France constituted a series of dynasties that could be traced back to the fifteenth century, as in the case of the Desfourneaux. Whoever the current headsman was, he came from a long line of men engaged in the same activities. In 1776 the executioner of Paris in theory was a seven-year-old boy, Charles Jean-Baptiste Sanson! At Epernay Simon Jean was only a little older when he fell heir to the title. Such lads were too young to perform such unsavoury tasks, so their guardians and uncles took over the role, guiding and instructing the novices until they reached manhood. Having entered into the profession, a family and its descendants were marked forever. There was no escaping their role; down through the generations brothers and sons were bound to the same employment and had to face the accompanying prejudice. The only friends, associates and potential spouses of an executioner were the families of other executioners.

Nicolas Roch continued to upgrade the guillotine in much the same way that Heindreicht had done. The machine was redesigned by aide Leon Berger. The old pulley system was replaced by a large pulley mounted on the top of the crossbar (*chapiteau*). On raising the blade to the summit of the machine an ingenious steel shaped arrowhead newly added to the *mouton* was forced into a tensioned grab that projected from inside the crossbar. The arrowhead and grab held the whole blade assembly in readiness at the summit of the machine. A quick downward pull on a lever attached to one of the side posts instantly opened the grab and allowed the whole mass to fall from its full height.

Roch retained the cosmetic changes introduced by his predecessor which lent the machine a degree of anonymity; he also, very considerately, went a stage further. During the year 1878 Roch informed the Abbé Crozes of La Roquette that his idea had been accepted. A large timber shield was attached to the uprights on the *bascule* side of the machine to further disguise the already blackened blade. With the knife in its ready position, it would thus be hidden from the view of the condemned on his approach to the guillotine. With this further refinement it could be fairly confidently asserted that the guillotine's victim neither saw nor felt a thing. He also dealt with another matter that had so far escaped the attention of the previous servants of the machine. As the *lunette* was closed to secure the victim's head, an iron grip was forcefully brought down at the same time, and post mortems revealed that this often caused minor fractures to the back of the head. Roch deemed this ancillary piece of equipment unnecessary and so dispensed with it. But what was this mysterious iron grip? Gordon Anderson of Los Angeles, the ultimate guillotineophile, solved the mystery. He has travelled the world searching out the secrets of the guillotine. His personal archives contain precise details of the construction of the machines used in France, Germany and Switzerland. He is a friend of Fernand Meyssonnier who was the executioner in Algeria.

The grip referred to was the steel arrowhead that surmounts the moution and fixes into the grab. On the original modern guillotine of 1868, the grab located in the top crossbeam (*chapiteau*) faced the *bascule* side of the machine. Since the arrowhead projected off the edge of the *mouton* it necessitated a notch to be cut in the centre of the upper *lunette*. It had to be deep enough so that the arrowhead would not strike the upper edge of the *lunette*. As the blade fell and compressed the shock absorbers, the notch in the centre allowed the fully depressed *mouton* to stay clear of the *lunette superior*'s edge and therefore not damage it. This construction can be clearly seen on the Algerian machine prior to its replacement with a repositioned grab assembly. Fernand Meyssonier the Algerian executioner knew of mishaps such as when the *mouton* fell on the *lunette* in its raised position completely smashing it and sending it out of the machine.

A blow from the debris striking the neck of the victim was more than capable of fracturing the occipital bone so Roch had its construction altered. The arrowhead and grab were moved to the opposite side making the slot in the upper *lunette* no longer necessary. The alteration ensured that the overhang of the arrowhead did not interfere with the operation of *lunette*. The guillotine of 1871 is often cited as being the first modernised version of the machine but this is incorrect. In fact the guillotine of 1868 sent to Algiers had all the new refinements fixed to it. It also included a uinque feature! The declic button was a sculpted bronze casting five inches in length. Shaped to resemble a decapitated torso wearing the traditional shirt cut away at the shoulders. This dark and humorous refinement was not repeated on the machines constructed after 1869.

The familiar sound of the double crash of the blade as it

fell and rebounded at the foot of the machine was also cut out. Roch installed heavy rubber shock absorbers to deal with the accumulated energy of the *mouton* as it fell, although this was of little consequence to the 'patient'. A further innovation was the installation of fitted parts to the machine which enabled the executioners to assemble it quietly. This way the condemned would no longer hear the dreadful hammering throughout the night forewarning him of his dawn rendezvous with the guillotine.

When Roch died in 1879, it was Anatole's father, Louis Deibler, who succeeded him. Of German extraction, Louis Deibler was a man who set great store by the traditions of the guillotine. With typical Teutonic zeal he did away with the Crozes and Roch blade mask, and the knife was restored to its original appearance, highly polished and shining. His guillotine reverted to its old, recognisable form, and that was how it remained until its abandonment over one hundred years later.

By the early 1870s the guillotine had reached a stage of practical excellence. From the summit of the machine the heavy blade would freefall between the uprights with a hollow roar in only three-quarters of a second, making light work of its grisly task. Like all mechanical devices the guillotine needed regular inspection and maintenance to ensure its proper functioning.

Let us now follow the executioner who will rendezvous with his aides on a certain weekday. In the confines of a prison, out of sight of its inmates, the inspection and assembly of the guillotine will take place. In a large hangar the machine lies unassembled, the uprights resting horizontally on three timber carpenter's horses. The four man team begin its assembly, working quietly and efficiently. First the base of the machine is laid in place and the cross members are connected together. Three assistants carry one of the posts into position onto the base. The chief executioner foots the base of the post whilst the three assistants under run it to the vertical position. The tongue on the bottom of the post is positioned into a groove on the base. Metal hinge plates attached to both the base and the bottom of the post are interlinked and a metal hinge pin in inserted to join post to base.

The second post is elevated in the same manner but before it is slotted into its rebate, the executioner lifts the heavy *mouton* into position and places it into the slide grooves. The second post is then dropped into its rebate and it too is secured with the heavy iron braces that have specially designed bolts.

Busying themselves in a most proficient manner two assistants fetch special scaling ladders with an extending cross piece attached to the head of the ladder, elevated, they are positioned to rest against the top of the posts. The *chapiteau* or top cross beam with its grab assembly fixed inside and surmounted by a pulley is then carried aloft and fitted over the posts. It also has a tongue and groove connection. The declic release bar that runs inside of one of the posts is bolted to the grab release lever inside the *chapiteau*. A metal door closes over the mechanism and is secured with a hasp and pin. A two inch hemp hawser is passed up the ladder and secured over the pulley. It will be used to haul the blade aloft. An iron cross member spans the two posts at a midway point and is bolted into position.

The assembly has almost been completed.

There is a hook fixed close to the arrowhed on top of the *mouton*. The rope is attached to it with a figure 8 metal ring. Through the centre of the ring is attached thin cord – a guy line that will be used to disengage the rope from the hook once the blade is in position and held by the grab. The blade will then freefall and not be hindered by the rope which is tucked to the side of the post.

The executioner has a wooden box that houses the blade and its three special bolts all numbered. Each bolt fixes through its own hole attaching the blade to the mouton. Raising the *mouton* off its buffers, the blade is bolted to the *mouton* then hauled aloft until the arrowhead locates into the grab.

The two sections of the *lunette* are then slid into position on the inside of the posts. They are heavy and covered on one side with shiny brass plate. The *lunette* switch and combined locking device is then screwed into position on the post.

The three sections of the bascule are fetched and fixed to the guillotine. First the upright support. Then the bed of the *bascule* with its rolling plank is fitted, supported by a post at one end and a bracket attached to the lower *lunette* at the other. The plank is tested to ensure it rolls freely towards the jaws of the guillotine. A second plank is secured to the side of the *bascule*. It droops at an angle and is used to tip the body from the machine into a large wicker container after an execution.

A couple more little more accessories are brought out of the hangar. A three-sided collapsible shield to protect 'the photographer' from blood splashes and a small metal bath that sits beneath the machine. The executioners stand back from the machine having removed the ladders. They look at the guillotine's potent imagery, a reflection of there own trade in sudden death. They are married to the widow and by tradition are deemed its servants!

The guillotine is a precision instrument. When the *lunette superior* is raised, it automatically locks into the open position. At the flick of a lever it descends with a loud bang on contact with the lower block and automatically locks shut.

A final test takes place. The fall of the cyclopean knife! The chief executioner satisfied that all is in readiness pulls down on the *manette*. The *declic* – the movement – frees the blade from the grab and with a muffled roar it slams down hard into the buffers. It is unbelievably quick. A head can be severed in a fraction of a second.

As casual observers, we can now leave the prison precincts, lost in silent approbation.

At a real execution, the chief executioner and his aides or valets were required to demonstrate a high level of competence when carrying out their duties. To this end, the chief executioner delegated specific responsibilities to his assistants. The least welcome task was that of 'photographer', whose duties had nothing to do with taking pictures. The photographer's duty was to ensure that once the victim's head was secured in the *lunette* he did not draw it back, which might result in the jaw or head being cut rather than the neck. Such a calamity occurred at the execution of triple murderer Louis Lefèvre at Tours on 10 June 1916. Before the fatal second, Lefèvre managed to pull his head free and back into the *lunette*. The result was that the blade sliced through the cranium instead of the neck. To prevent such catastrophes, the assistant was required to stand at the head side of the guillotine and if necessary pull the victim forward by the hair or ears to ensure he was in the correct position for the blade to do its work. A mutilated patient would not be applauded by the ever-critical audience. As this assistant was concerned with settling the victim in the right pose, he became known in criminal jargon as 'the photographer'. His position relative to the unfortunate victim meant that he would often become saturated with blood. Limited protection was afforded against this by the 'photographer's shield' that was placed between the victim's head and the assistant.

* * *

The decree of 25 November 1870 would change forever the lives of the famous executing families. From this point there would be only one national executioner for the whole of France. In the executioners' heyday the brotherhood numbered 160, but from the end of the revolutionary period onwards this number had been whittled down to just a few. From 1870 only one Monsieur de Paris would be responsible for the decapitation of all the nation's felons, irrespective of where the executions were scheduled to take place.

Had Clément-Henri Sanson not fallen from favour, he might well have been appointed to this exalted position, even at the age of seventy-two. In fact he lived to the ripe old age of ninety, and as executioners seldom retired he might have continued the trade for another eighteen years. However, it was not to be, and Clément-Henri was much relieved when he was replaced by Férey. Eight years later in 1849, the famous Heindreicht took over and after his death, Nicolas Roch became chief executioner.

Following Roch's death in 1879, a new dynasty of executioners appeared on the scene. The Deiblers' name would become as familiar as the Sansons' and would be synonymous with the guillotine itself. Breaking with tradition, the new executioners were not related to any of the revolutionary or earlier dynasties. Ironically, they were not even French but German, and with typical Teutonic resolve continued a three-generation career that would eventually remove nearly two thousand heads from their rightful owners. The Deiblers would be the last upholders of the hereditary tradition that handed down the role of chief executioner from father to son.

Joseph-Antoine Deibler was born in Bavaria in 1789, at the beginning of the French Revolution. Following the defeat of Napoleon at Waterloo, the 27-year-old Deibler found himself in France as a member of the allied occupation forces. Enjoying his situation in a new country, he decided to settle down and commenced a new and happy existence as the owner of a small wine shop in Lyon. In 1817 the executioner in Dijon, Antoine Desmorets, required an assistant, and Joseph Deibler sold his wine shop and moved to Dijon to begin a new career as a guillotiner. As Antoine's apprentice, Joseph was to prove himself more than capable and remained in service alongside his mentor until 1847. Their working relationship was very successful, tutor and student becoming good friends as well as mutually respectful colleagues. Joseph even named his new-born son after his employer. Louis Antoine Stanislas Deibler was born on 13 February 1823.

Joseph Deibler's talents in the execution business may not have been mere chance. There was an interesting family connection with the craft, as his grandfather had been the town's executioner at Biberach in Germany. One wonders if this inspired him to try this new career. Perhaps the young Deibler went on exciting trips with his grandfather to the Nuremberg Torture Museum, where his enquiring and impressionable mind eagerly absorbed his grandfather's explanations of the workings of the iron maiden, the spikes, the hatchets and the gibbets.

Many years later Joseph's own son Louis dreamed of an interesting career outside the sphere of the *bourreau* and the guillotine, but this was not to be and was regarded as simply a pipe dream. Whether he wished it or not, the young

Louis was heir apparent to the Deibler dynasty. Hemmed in by his father's profession, Louis found that his destiny was already marked out. Fortunately his training was supervised not only by his ageing father but also by the magnificent Desmorets, whose family had sprung to prominence as executioners during the Revolution.

In 1853 Joseph, now a sprightly sixty-four and with some thirty-five years of experience in the trade, left France for Algiers. He was accompanied by his wife Marguerite and his son Louis, now a grown man of thirty. When the family arrived they were met and made welcome by Antoine Rasseneux, another patron and servant of the guillotine, which was still at work in Algiers. The headsmen of France could be likened to a masonic order, always looking after their own. It is likely that the move to Algiers had been primarily undertaken in order to find a bride for Louis. As far as the executioners and their aides were concerned, Louis was a prince among headsmen and a very eligible bachelor. It so happened that Antoine Rasseneux's attractive daughter was only eighteen years old, and the stigma of her father's profession meant she would be unlikely to find a suitor from respectable society. Louis, similarly limited in the choice of a potential spouse, quickly succumbed to the charming and attractive Mademoiselle Zoë, encouraged by the conniving Joseph and Antoine. Within a year Louis and Zoë were married.

In executing circles the union between a Rasseneux and a Deibler was warmly welcomed and the elderly but still active Joseph could now dream of a grandson to carry on the family tradition. Back home in France, the ailing Desmorets sadly passed away without being reunited with the Deiblers. His post was left vacant. Joseph Deibler was duly promoted to the post of Monsieur de Rennes and was nominated as chief executioner for the western departments. Having no reason at all for remaining away from home, the family returned to France. Louis and Zoë's fruitful union produced four children in as many years, the first and only one to survive being Anatole Joseph. The three remaining children, Berthe, Algae and Ernest, all died before reaching the age of five years. A similar fate awaited Anatole's own child many years later. Old Joseph, in the happy twilight years of his life, died content in the knowledge that his son would carry on the family tradition, and his grandson too if all went well.

In 1870 Louis was forty-seven and still in the prime of his professional life. Young Anatole was almost eight years old and thriving. The Deiblers had a modest but comfortable lifestyle that was to improve as time went by. Anatole even purchased his own automobile and posed for a picture in it with his wife. Louis's commitment to and proficiency in his important post did not go unnoticed by the Establishment. As soon as the remaining provincial executioners were forcibly retired by the authority of the 1870 decree, he was nominated to be retained as assistant to Nicolas Roch.

The admirable Roch's reign ended with his death in 1879 and the equally admirable Louis Deibler, previously assistant executioner at Rennes, became the national executioner for France and Algeria at the relatively young age of fifty-five. Anatole had grown into an attractive young man who would somewhat reticently follow in his father's footsteps. Their fame was promoted in due course by their involvement in the execution of a number of notorious murderers and other criminals: the legendary anarchist Ravachol, the notorious Bluebeard Henri Désiré Landru, the sadistic serial killer Joseph Vacher and the bandits of Hazebrouck, Auguste and Abel Pollet.

Louis was not immune to criticism from the public. Older members of his audiences could look back to a time when executions were carried out far more expeditiously. Louis had gained a reputation as a 'slow' executioner, sometimes taking a whole minute to dispatch a felon. Those who could remember the amazing speed of the record breakers such as Heindreicht and Roch were vociferously contemptuous of the new master, the most severe critics being Messrs Grison and Dornain. For poor Louis, distressed by the verbal assaults of his impertinent critics, it was all too much. He was accused of being too clumsy, imprecise and lacking assurance; he was too gentle and he was too rough; he was too nervous and worst of all he was too slow.

Of all these gibes it was the accusation of slowness that most annoyed Deibler. Every executioner had a duty to ensure the safety of his team members. On one occasion in 1829 one of Henri Sanson's assistants moved too slowly away from the machine – and lost three fingers as the blade flashed down.

He was also accused by his critics of displaying too much prissiness and gentlemanly conduct in the time-consuming act of arranging the victim upon the *bascule* – but this was the same Louis Deibler who only four days after his appointment as national executioner was accused of Azilian tendencies. He had been forced to strike the head of an unwilling victim upon the pavement in order to overcome the man's resistance and keep control of the situation. As M. Grison might have said, disapprovingly: 'This would never have happened in Heindreicht's day!' In 1882, at the guillotining of the parricide Pierre Lanz, also witnessed by the critical Grison, it took Deibler more than a minute to settle Lanz on the machine. 'Outrageous! Why, Roch would have completed it in ten seconds.'

Such meaningless comparisons serve little purpose, as the average time to complete an execution once the victim had reached the foot of the guillotine was between fifteen and twenty seconds. Indeed, Louis's son Anatole was applauded in the press when he presided over a quadruple execution in 1909, completing the task in a little under nine minutes. The offenders were members of a gang that had been terrorising the inhabitants of the northern districts of Picardy and Artois. They had been apprehended in 1908. Brothers Auguste and Abel Pollet both perished on the guillotine, along with Canut Vromant and Théophile Deroo. The executions were witnessed by a journalist from the Pathé-Journal newsreel company and despite the governments attempts to prevent it, on this occasion were allegedly filmed. This macabre piece of cinema if it exists has never apparently been located. The Minister of the Interior immediately took steps to prevent such an occurrence happening again, and filming of the guillotine was prohibited, including simulated or acted executions in which the guillotine was visible.

The Guillotine and the Executioners

Twenty-five years later the attitude of the French government had not changed. Any display of the guillotine was simply not permitted, which was rather ridiculous since all executions still took place in public. In 1934 French cinema-goers who went to see the film *The Scarlet Pimpernel* with Leslie Howard in the title role saw a heavily censored version from which the guillotine had been removed. There was also a protest over the film *Devil's Island* with Boris Karloff, made in 1940, in which the guillotine made two appearances. The drama of the final scene is intense as the blade falls and becomes wedged just inches from Karloff's shrinking neck, his head still secured in the collar of the machine. The film was considered to be making a political statement condemning the penal conditions in French Guiana, known as the 'dry guillotine'.

A triple execution of the Chauffeurs de la Drôme also took place at Valence on 22 September 1909. Despite the edict prohibiting the publication of pictures of the machine, an enterprising photographer surreptitiously managed to take a series of photographs of these executions, one of which showed the blade in mid-course. The pictures were made into a set of picture postcards and sold commercially. Clearly people were still fascinated by the guillotine.

In 1892 Louis Deibler had another seven years to serve as the chief executioner. If, as his disdainful critics had suggested, he displayed a sense of nervousness and unease in fulfilling his duties, then between the years 1892 and 1894 it was not without good reason. For the first time in the history of the guillotine the executioner's impartiality was brought into question. It was an era of anarchy, in which France became paranoid about internal terrorism. Once again the class struggle between poverty and wealth was seen as resolvable only through violence. In a comfortable bourgeois existence the greatest perceived dangers to the status quo were the liberal anti-hero and the anarchist. For the next three years the guillotine and the executioner were seen as the tools of a corrupt form of bourgeois control and persecution, defending the rights and interests of the ruling classes against the poor, downtrodden and ultimately despised proletariat. With the increase in the anarchical tendencies of a few devoted anti-heroes and assassins, the government fought back through the offices of the bourreau and the guillotine, ultimately demeaning the role of the headsman.

For the anarchists, their actions were intended to herald the winds of change, ultimately ushering in a new age of true equality and real freedom. The fact that a small number of innocent people would have to be sacrificed for the cause was considered a small price to pay for mankind's realisation of the dream of liberty and happiness. The city of Paris fell victim to a continuous series of bomb attacks. François Claudius Koenigstein, known as Ravachol, was the first of four terrorists to face the guillotine between the years 1892 and 1894. Condemned to death for murder, he was also labelled by the authorities a graverobber, thief and counterfeiter. Supported by the political far left, Ravachol was hailed as a saint and a defender of the downtrodden. His death was acclaimed as a sort of martyrdom and quickly turned him into a legendary figure of fantasy violence. Undoubtedly charismatic, his objectives in his own words were: 'To terrorise and so force society to look attentively at those who suffer.' Ravachol, the anarchist and atheist, went to the guillotine on 11 July 1892 singing an anti-religious song, confident that his death would soon be avenged.

When Louis Deibler was ordered to proceed with the execution there was little doubt in his mind that the widespread popularity of the rebellious anarchist would encourage people to view the executioner not as a neutral functionary, simply carrying out his duty as an extension of justice, but as a tool of nefarious and scheming politicians. The anarchist movement decided to attack the rule of law at the sharp end, and began a campaign of intimidation against the already apprehensive bourreau and his guillotine. After all, if there was no headsman, then there could be no execution. The warnings to Deibler came in a series of intimidating letters. Should the execution take place, then he would be targeted for revenge and reprisals. The threats were dire and warned of torture and murder. The limited prestige of the worried executioner had already been severely eroded by scathing attacks from the radical periodicals that sympathised with the terrorists' objectives. As the conflict heated up, the government prepared to make a large number of arrests and also to enforce new laws which would close down many of the left-wing newspapers. Deibler's fears may not have been misplaced. Fernand Meyssonnier the Algerian executioner in conversaation with Gordon Anderson related the events that occurred in Algeria. Meyssonnier's father had also been chief executioner and was caught and tortured by dissidents. An assistant to his father was also killed in a bomb attack.

The anarchists continued to prey on the executioner's nervous disposition and even expanded their campaign of threats to include Deibler's landlord. Should Ravachol's head fall, then the executioner's pleasant home in the rue d'Azir would be bombed. The threat was not taken lightly, and the unhappy bourreau was dispossessed of his home by an equally frightened and unhappy landlord.

None of the threats was carried out. The execution took place without incident on 11 July 1892. A little more than a century before, the Bastille had been stormed, signalling the beginning of the Revolution. The Revolution of 1789 brought down an ancient and formidable institution. Now the bourgeois establishment was to destroy a new stock of Revolutionaries using the same terrible machine that had been used against them, and there would be no quarter.

Ravachol's threat of revenge and further violence was not an idle one. The guillotine and the likelihood of execution did not deter further outbreaks of terrorism. In 1893 22-year-old Auguste Vaillant threw a bomb from the visitors' gallery into the Chamber of Deputies. Through chance and good fortune, there were no fatalities. Vaillant was apprehended, tried and convicted. For the first time in the nineteenth century the guillotine would be used as a political weapon, and the blade would fall upon those who were neither murderers nor traitors. The agitated Deibler was again the target of death threats. His life was threatened if and when Vaillant was executed. As apprehensive as before, Deibler was forced to carry out his function at the cost of his own safety. Vaillant marched to the guillotine without any expression of fear. He had refused the counsel of a priest and declined the customary offering of Cognac. All his senses remained acute, right to the second that Deibler's blade sliced through his neck on 5 February 1894.

If Ravachol was deemed a saviour by his followers, then the courageous Vaillant was his principal disciple. In the minds of the radicals both men had become sacrificial martyrs dedicated to freedom in the struggle against bourgeois domination. Vaillant's blood-soaked remains were placed into small receptacles and 'sanctified' as relics of the great cause, the struggle against oppression, for which both men had forfeited their lives.

Five months later the actions of Ravachol and Vaillant were overshadowed by the activities of another anarchist, Emile Henry. The time had come for another outrage to be perpetrated against the Establishment in the name of freedom. Emile was a mere eighteen years of age, belligerent and filled with hatred for the bourgeois society that once again dominated France. His father had fled to Spain to escape the death sentence imposed upon many of the Communards. Emile, an irrational and ruthless young man inspired by the actions of Ravachol and Auguste Vaillant, had been brought up on a diet of insurgence and confrontation. His absence of conscience and warped thinking meant he did not hesitate when he threw a bomb into the busy Café Terminus at Gare St-Lazare. His only regret was that the explosion had killed only one person. This misguided idealist would also pay the extreme penalty for his action. Like Ravachol and Vaillant, he went to his death shouting 'Long live anarchy,' and seemed not to notice the guillotine.

For Emile Henry's execution on 21 May 1894, the government ensured a dominant police and military presence to maintain order and also to send out a clear message to the brotherhood that the only reward for anarchy was the guillotine. Louis Deibler, still anxious about the threats hanging over him but reassured by the large police presence, guillotined the young terrorist without incident. By August 1894 the anarchists would have disappeared like an early morning mist, leaving nothing to posterity or to progress. Louis and his guillotine could then revert to decapitating those members of society that society reviled, but first there would be one more act of supreme anarchy.

President Sadi Carnot (President of France from 1887 to 1894) was among the thousands who flocked to Lyons to visit the Universal Exhibition. In what seemed to be a spontaneous act of violence, he was stabbed to death by a twenty-year-old baker's apprentice named Santo Hierominus Casério. This was to be the last and perhaps most damaging act of blatant terrorism suffered by the government. The response was swift and inevitable, and another young misfit was sentenced to the guillotine.

It became obvious to the supporters of chaos that stronger and more drastic measures would have to be taken to dissuade the *bourreau* from executing Casério. Intimidating letters did not have the desired effect. Two days after the execution of Emile Henry, Louis Deibler was walking alone when he was snatched from the street. Dazed by a blow to the head, he was forcibly bundled into a waiting vehicle. His struggles to escape and his shouts for help brought several members of the public running to his aid. Dragged out of the van as unceremoniously as he had been thrown into it, the now truly intimidated *bourreau* had all his worst fears confirmed. The gendarmerie subsequently provided him with a guard and carried out a number of raids within the district to ensure that their presence was felt and to prevent any similar incidents occurring in future.

Casério was duly guillotined at Lyons, but the twenty-year-old was unable to demonstrate the same vociferous courage and fortitude displayed by his predecessors. Trembling with fright he was allegedly carried to the guillotine, and screamed in terror as the blade was released. Not to demean the anarchist legend of courage and defiance in the shadow of the guillotine, rumour circulated that Caserio's last gesture to the government that had codemned him was a shout of, 'Courage comrades, long live anarchy!'

An ill-looking Deibler had survived his personal ordeal and the Establishment had triumphed over dissidence. The left-wing radical journals continued to be hounded and closed down, and more arrests were made, but Parisian society could at last breathe again. Louis Deibler thanked God for looking after him and was seen on a pilgrimage to Lourdes. He regularly attended his local church, though his conscience prevented him from ever approaching the altar without gloved hands – which to date had removed over sixty-six heads as France's national executioner.

Louis had been engaged in his trade for half a century. He was now aged seventy-four and had begun to suffer from the executioner's nightmare, the ignominious trait of haemophobia, a morbid fear of blood. It was clearly time for him to step down, the long years of lopping off heads having taken their toll. He was indeed only half the man he had been, and, like Clément-Henri Sanson five decades before, he too would be glad to relinquish his vocation. The old headsman was tormented in his waking hours and equally tortured in his sleep. He suffered from vivid nightmares and, in his waking hours, in a gesture curiously reminiscent of Pontius Pilate, Louis continuously and mechanically dry-washed his hands, attempting to cleanse himself from the invisible flood of blood that represented his life's work. In old age the psychological scars of his craft were plainly visible and no human reassurance could retrieve his diminishing sanity.

In 1897 Louis had guillotined a criminal named Dominique Harsch, the murderer of 15 year old Margot Fiesch in the town of Nancy. As the head fell into the basket, the blood pumping from the severed neck spurted forward more than two metres from the machine, saturating Louis's clothing. For him it was the final straw. The chief executioner was reduced to a trembling pathetic old man. At an execution a year later on 25 June 1898 Louis foundered again under the illusion that he had been covered in the blood of the victim Xavier Carrara. His time was at its end. In over fifty years beside the guillotine, Louis had seen one thousand heads fall. Within another twelve months he was to make his farewell performance before an exuberant crowd. Though he was officiating at this execution, it was his son Anatole who attended to the formalities of decapitating the sadist Joseph Vacher on 31 December 1898 at Bourg en Bresse.

As a young man Anatole had hoped to escape his father's profession and tried to disassociate himself from the guillotine by seeking employment elsewhere. Like others who had tried before, he failed, although he managed to escape temporarily by joining a regiment. At that time he frequently assisted his father at executions. However, it was not long before his identity came to light. He was distrusted by his colleagues and subjected to discrimination; some, quite without reason, even feared him. Eventually he was forced to leave his regiment and found employment working in a department store, this time using an alias. His disguise did not work, however, and again he was recognised. Isolated and spurned by his peers, all that was left for him was to rejoin his father as an assistant in 1882.

Anatole was to become the first twentieth-century headsman and would remain in the post of chief executioner for forty years. Executioners and their assistants had always been exempt from military service, as they were considered an essential link in the chain of justice. Even in times of national emergency, crime and punishment still prevailed. Criminals subject to military control were executed by firing squad while those who were condemned by the civil authorities had to face the guillotine.

Like so many executioners before him, Anatole experienced great difficulty in finding a wife outside the profession. He attempted to win the hand of Mlle Herteloup, his first love, but he was unable to overcome the old prejudices and secure her father's permission to marry her, despite the fact that her bigoted and hypercritical father, M. Herteloup, was a carpenter who actually constructed the guillotines.

Obviously believing that the man who used his product was too lowly for his daughter, he resolutely refused to allow the marriage to proceed.

Anatole eventually married Rosalie Rogis, who had links with various past executioners. Rosalie's brother Louis was to become an assistant executioner to Anatole, while her sister was the mother of André Obrecht, a future chief executioner from 1951 until 1976. André's cousin Georgette married Henri Desfourneaux, who became chief executioner after Anatole's death in 1939. It was Henri who performed the very last public execution in France, that of the serial killer Eugène Weidmann outside the St-Pierre prison at Versailles on 17 June 1939.

Anatole and Rosalie's married life was not without tragedy. Their son Roger Isidore died at the age of five as a result of a pharmacist's mistake in prescribing him medicine, and when their daughter Marcelle fell in love with her cousin André, she was forbidden to marry the future headsman, for obvious reasons. As the nineteenth century closed and the twentieth opened, a newspaper wrote of the new Monsieur de Paris the following enthusiastic and complimentary statement:

All the newspapers agree in paying tribute to young M. Deibler [Anatole was then thirty-eight years old] whose Paris debut showed a handiness and ease of an old practitioner. Youthful, elegant, dressed in a frock coat of sombre hue, like a second at some exclusive duel, he typifies the modern executioner. After this happy beginning, one can safely predict for him a fine career and respectable number of performances.

Throughout the careers of successive executioners, their dress and mannerisms were the object of careful scrutiny by a curious public. During the revolutionary years it became fashionable to dress like Charles-Henri Sanson with a tricorn hat, a coat of dark green – a redingcote with cut-away front of contrasting colour – and striped trousers. The elegant Nicolas Roch donned a top hat and frock coat. Louis Deibler, similarly attired, always carried with him a black umbrella and Anatole eventually exchanged the top hat for a derby, which no doubt promoted the sales of this new article of headgear.

The executioners' pariah-like status grossly misrepresented their true nature and standing. They were not, as was imagined, sinister, vile or vulgar. Their hands were not coarse or ingrained with the clotted and hardened residues of blood spilled from so many executions. They were ordinary men, and yet at the same time they were extraordinary. The Sansons, for example, like their latter-day counterparts, were educated middle-class members of society. Most could speak English, enjoyed music, were devoted to their families and were never less than model civil servants. The contrast between their personal attributes and their deadly function, however, was always puzzling.

Anatole Deibler was officially the national executioner from 1899 until 1939, the year of his death. His accession was greeted by the public with favour, although he would prove to be the last member of an executing dynasty. With the dawning of the twentieth century and Anatole's appointment, it seemed as if the executioner was at last rehabilitated into polite society.

Throughout the guillotine's dark history, the executioner and his machine had no real official status in the political sphere. The executioner and his machine was an enigma shrouded in mystery and seldom referred to. Even the word guillotine was omitted from the French statutes. There was never any description of the appointee's duties or responsibilities. Unlike the latter-day British hangmen, there was no training or examination to prove at least a theoretical knowledge of the procedures and efficiency required in the state-sponsored art of killing. Those condemned to death by the Republic were abandoned by it. The victims of the guillotine were subcontracted out to the executioner and in their final hour became his property, to be disposed of by him in accordance with law and tradition. Whenever a new executioner was selected, he was usually sought from among the existing dynasties.

Guillotine

The executioner's golden age had obviously been during the Revolution. At that time they had been granted full rights of citizenship for the first time, and their craft was deemed a national duty. The somewhat derogatory title *'bourreau'* was prohibited, and they became the avengers of the people. The fear and prejudice so often levelled against them disappeared, for it was now 'the Timbers of Justice' that killed, painlessly and effortlessly. Now, at the dawn of the twentieth century, Anatole Deibler could feel the warm glow of appreciation bestowed by press and public alike on their new impresario of death. Society continued to use the guillotine to rid itself of transgressors against the law while maintaining the concept of human dignity that originally created it. This same concept of human dignity would in later years radically change and would eventually provide the basis for a challenge to the very existence of the machine.

Opposition to the guillotine had already successfully removed the spectacle from an execution by abolishing the scaffold. With the theatre gone, it was also drained of its ceremonial aspect. The next major task was to extinguish its cultural popularity by removing the crowds. This would not be achieved until 1939. Once the guillotine had been robbed of its audience, the movement supporting its abolition could focus the idea in the public mind that the now-antiquated machine was little better than a tool for brutal, state-inspired murders inflicted upon the insane and helpless. Once this was accepted in principle, the days remaining to the guillotine would be numbered.

All of this lay in the future when Anatole Deibler became chief executioner. For the moment the guillotine and its servants remained in the ascendant. Following the execution of Damoiseau at Troyes on the 14 January, a confident Anatole, neatly bearded, well dressed and of good demeanour, made his official debut in the capital on 1 February 1899, guillotining the nineteen-year-old murderer Alfred Peugnez. Witnessing this auspicious event was the former prime minister of Great Britain, the 5th Earl of Rosebery. It was the last execution outside of La

Roquette. One week later he travelled to Remiremont to guillotine Aloïs Zuckermeyer another child murderer.

Anatole was not a novice at the time of his appointment; he had been an assistant to his father for at least seven years. He was also accompanied by experienced aides, men like Desmorets, Berger and Desfourneaux. Any one of them would have been equally qualified to perform the role of principal executioner, but in keeping with tradition the state chose Anatole.

In 1918, towards the end of the First World War, the Belgian government requested the services of an executioner and guillotine for the execution of Camille Verfuille. Although capital punishment had been abolished in Belgium over half a century before, the politicians wanted to make an example of Verfuille for his savage murder of a young servant-girl Rachel Rykerwaert. The execution was scheduled to take place in the market-place at Furnes, but because of a German bombardment at Adinkerque and Furnes the executioner and his aides were forced to take shelter for several hours. Why Verfuille could not simply have been executed by means of a firing squad, rather than going to all the trouble of borrowing a guillotine and executioners from France, is not known. Of course, the guillotine had been used in Belgium prior to the abolition of capital punishment, and this may account for the decision. The execution was finally carried out, not in public as was planned, but hastily within the confines of the prison as a result of further bombardment from the German forces. A rather shaken crew returned to Paris with their machine, complaining that they had been sent into a battlefield. As executioners they were obviously acclimatised to only one kind of abrupt death, from the fall of the blade and not the bomb.

This was not the first time or the last that the guillotine travelled outside France. In 1793 it could be found in the West Indies and in 1798 in Belgium. It was also used in northern Italy and in some German states, Bavaria, Saxony Wuertemberg and the Rhine province. In 1833 it found a home in Greece when two assassins were guillotined at Thebes and in 1859 travelled from the French post of Martinque to Newfoundland. In 1864 the guillotine was used in Tahiti to execute two Chinese at Papeete. In 1910 the Chinese ordered a French guillotine which was soon made operative, and in the same year, the last public execution took place in Sweden, when Alfred Anders was guillotined on 23 November.

In 1930 in Indo China (present day Vietnam), thirteen nationalists were guillotined on the same day. The machine had arrived at the beginning of the twentieth century and was last used in 1960 for the execution of Hoang Kha, a member of the communist party. From 1848 the guillotine was used in Algeria, the last execution taking place in 1959. Also Madagascar in 1956.

In Nazi dominated Germany a redesigned guillotine was used aiding the spread of tyranny. Adolph Hitler ordered the construction of a further twenty guillotines to quell members of the populace that opposed the Nazi regime. The guillotines were dispersed to prisons throughout Germany, Austria and Czechoslovakia.

Anatole Deibler officiated at the execution of the notorious 'Bluebeard', Henri Desiré Landru, in 1922. Landru had begun his life of crime as a petty criminal. His wayward character was thought to be responsible for precipitating his father's suicide. Progressing from petty crime to murder proved an easy step for him and in 1915 he murdered Jeanne Cuchet and her seventeen-year-old son, disposing of their bodies in the hearth of their home. Jeanne Cuchet had met Landru through the agency of a lonely hearts column in a newspaper. The romance culminated in the unfortunate woman signing over all of her wealth and possessions to the bearded Romeo. In the same year another two murders were committed. Moving to Gambais, the charming Bluebeard caused the disappearance of a further seven women. Landru was finally arrested on 12 April 1919 following a police investigation into his numerous missing ladyfriends. The investigation was instigated by the Mayor of Gambais. In the isolated country cottage that Landru had rented in Gambais, police discovered more than 290 bone fragments, teeth, personal possessions and clothes from his victims. The human remains were found in the deposits of ash inside the house stove. The exact number of his victims was never known. In November 1921 in the Seine-et-Oise he was found guilty of murder and was guillotined on 25 February 1922. At dawn on that day, as the prison gates opened, he walked with a firm step towards the guillotine. Between his first appearance at the gates and his death just twenty-six seconds elapsed.

Landru never admitted his guilt to anyone but continued to protest his innocence to the end. Thirty-eight years later, in 1963, the daughter of the defence counsel who had represented Landru at his trial had a small picture removed from its frame for cleaning. It had belonged to her father and had been given to him by Landru while he was awaiting his execution. Hidden behind the picture was a single line written in Landru's own hand: 'I did it. I burned their bodies in my kitchen oven.' He had confessed at last.

Anatole's career had begun with the execution of Vacher, though technically, his father was present at the execution and deemed to be in charge, and he went on to remove from society many other notorious criminals. In his forty years in office he was to carry out some 395 executions. From the outset he tried to make the post of executioner more acceptable, removing the ancient stigma associated with the profession of the headsman. In short Anatole Deibler was a consummate professional and on the public platform it seemed he had style. Modest, conscientious, professional and respected, what more could be expected of an executioner? His colleague and brother-in-law Louis Rogis held him in the highest esteem, and they spent many off-duty hours together playing billiards at the Café Marseille among their friends and acquaintances. At the end of his career with his health failing him, he was unable to attend to the execution of Lucien Boulay the murderer of little nine year old Therese Rouaultat. On 13 January 1938, Henri Desfourneaux took care of these formalities at Saint-Brieuc. Eleven days later with Anatole feeling a little better, he was able to guillotine Abdelkader Rakida in the town of Lyon. It was to be his 395 execution and 299 as chief. Unknown to him it was also to be his last.

On 2 February 1939 Anatole set out for Rennes, where his grandfather Joseph Deibler had begun the family tradition more than a century before. His journey was undertaken not for social or sentimental reasons but for business. The murderer Pilorges was sentenced to be guillotined. But en route, Anatole Deibler, now an old man of seventy-six, collapsed in the Métro station from a fatal heart attack, bringing to an end the reign of the Deiblers. He was succeeded by a nephew through marriage, Henri Desfourneaux, who was himself sixty-two. The death of the chief executioner did not delay the execution for too long. Two days later Maurice Pilorges, a cut throat had his rendezvous with Desforneaux and a different kind of razor! Many years later in 2003 Anatole Deibler's diaries in the form of fourteen notebooks were auctioned in Paris for the amazing sum of 66,110 euros. The notebooks listed an account of each execution he carried out. Details of their trials, their behaviour on the fatal day and even the weather conditions. All listed by the man that severed nearly 300 heads as chief executioner. Clearly, the fascination with the guillotine outlived the machine's own saturnine history. In the year of Anatole's death Nazi Germany would use its new form of warfare, the Blitzkrieg, to overrun western Europe in the blink of an eye and engage the western Allies in six years of war that would change the face of the world.

Desfourneaux's lineage could be traced back to medieval times and he was undoubtedly considered a fitting replacement for the late Anatole Deibler. A little over four months after Deibler's death Desfourneaux was to execute Eugène Weidmann. This was to be his only performance before a public audience as chief executioner, though he had carried out two previous executions before ratification of his appointment. Eight days later, on 26 June 1939, the guillotine in Paris would be relegated to the confines of the Santé prison, where henceforth all future executions in Paris would take place. On the day that Weidmann was guillotined a slight miscalculation meant that the execution occurred during daylight hours rather than at dawn. Weidmann had not been correctly 'arranged' on the guillotine until the third attempt, thus slowing down the execution. Though film evidence seems contrary to this. However, there is a photograph that indicates Weidmann's determination not to go to his death like a lamb to the slaughter. Struggling, his body is out of alignemnt with the forward thrust of the *bascule*. This very minor delay allowed news photographers located in an upstairs room of a nearby building to take clear pictures of the execution. One of the photographs shows the blade about to be released by Desfourneaux. An aide has grasped Weidmann by the ankles, preventing him from moving while prostrate on the *bascule*. Another aide steadies the torso. With Weidmann's head secured in the *lunette*, the 'photographer' André Obrecht, has stepped back from the machine before the fatal second. The position taken up by the 'photographer' in relation to a successful execution was an importamt one. At the Weidmann execution, the protocol seems not to have been observed as he has clearly stepped well back from the guillotine. At the side of the guillotine there is a wicker container, its lid open, waiting to receive the headless corpse. The large crowd of onlookers, kept back behind a police cordon, appears subdued and well behaved, in contradiction of later government reports of rowdiness and bad behaviour. The picture adds solemnity to the occasion. But this crowd was only the inner circle. Further back behind a police cordon was a second crowd that indeed did relegate themselves to rowdiness and bad behaviour some dipping their handerkerchiefs into the spilled blood. In France, rare photographs of the execution were published in the June 1939 issue of 'Detective magazine'. The day after the execution the photograph, the last of its kind, appeared with others in the *Paris Soir* newspaper. The government, unamused, accused the press of bowing to the voyeuristic and sadistic inclinations of their readers and justifiably used the incident as a reason for abandoning public executions forever. The final link in the counter-guillotine movement's chain had been forged. The guillotine was finally robbed of its last macabre tradition: it had been denied its audience. Desfourneaux's next execution, that of Jean Dehaene occurred behind prison walls at Saint-Brieuc on the 19th July 1939. It was the first execution without a public audience.

In the wake of the Second World War the executioner's status, carefully preserved and indeed rehabilitated by Anatole Deibler, was again to decline. It had always been the duty of the executioner to decapitate those condemned by the law impartially and irrespective of which faction held the reins of power. This was never better demonstrated than by the great Sanson. The executioner appointed by the king, he then executed the king, who had been condemned by the Revolution. The Revolution's power-mongers in their turn became Sanson's victims on the orders of the moderates, who in turn were replaced by another king. The king was then replaced by an emperor and then by another republic. Sanson guillotined all who were sent to him with as little unpleasantness as possible and remained in his post. There was never any suggestion of reprisal against the executioner, whose neutrality was considered beyond question. Henri Desfourneaux was to demonstrate the same impartiality throughout the precarious years of the German occupation of France, but the stress associated with maintaining such impartiality would take its toll on him.

In the week before the victorious Nazi armies marched into Paris in June 1940, Desfourneaux guillotined a German citizen named Fritz Erler, condemned to death as a spy. Erler's accomplice Carmen Mory was condemned with him. Mory, notorious later for her bestial cruelty, was known as the Black Angel of Ravensbruck. Her death sentence, in accordance with tradition, was rescinded, leaving Erler to face the guillotine alone, had it not been for the murderer Maurice Garnotal who after a struggle with the executioners was guillotined the same morning. Since all political prisoners were normally shot by firing squad, the German authorities complained strongly to the French, not about the execution in itself but against the method used to carry it out.

In Nazi Germany Adolf Hitler saw the guillotine as an ignoble and degenerate form of execution. Notwithstanding this, the conquering German forces of the occupation accepted the executioner as a neutral functionary, a man untainted by such delicate issues as collaboration or, worse, active resistance. He would be allowed to continue through the Occupation and afterwards, perhaps the only government official who was instinctively placed beyond doubt. Whether Desfourneaux wished it or not, he was to serve the collaborationist French regime just as he would have served any other. He was to execute the usual supply of muderers, then between 1942 and 1944 fifteen communists (nine of them on one day) and even five members of the French Resistance who were condemned as German reprisals for the slaying of Nazis in occupied France. One of them Marcel Langer was chief of the south west faction of the resistance and was guillotined on the 23 July 1943. Such actions incensed the assistant executioners who withdrew their services until hostilities ceased. On 5 November 1943, André Obrecht, Georges Martin and Robert Martin relinquished their posts until 1945. However, their vacated positions were quickly filled by other assistants.

For the first time in France since 1887, women were again sent to the guillotine. Between the years 1887 and 1941 women sentenced to death were automatically pardoned and their sentence commuted to imprisonment. Louis Deibler, the last headsman to guillotine a woman, became so distraught and emotionally unnerved by the incident that he said he would rather resign his position than have to do it again. Desfourneaux, perhaps of stronger temperament, executed three women between 1941 and 1943. All were condemned by Marshal Pétain's Vichy government. During the war years the collaborationist regime passed harsh laws of a puritanical nature to encourage higher moral values and family virtues. Revolutionary equality for all men and women had returned with a vengeance. A new law prohibiting abortion resulted in the execution of the last of the three women, Marie-Louise Giraud, a back-street abortionist who was guillotined on 30 July 1943 at La Roquette. She did not go to her death quietly, but screaming, fighting and swearing. She was the mother of two children but this did not save her.

Desfourneaux's impartiality may have been only skin deep, for his years as an executioner took a heavy toll upon his mental state. He was aware that his strict neutrality had compelled him to guillotine many innocent people along with the guilty. When France was again free, he and his aides were eventually acquitted of all charges of complicity and collaboration with the enemy, though by now the executioner's reputation was beyond salvage. In 1946 Henri Desfourneaux continued where he had left off, as chief executioner of the Fourth Republic of France. In that year the guillotine was to embrace Dr Marcel Petiot, one of the most notorious murderers in the annals of French criminal history, a precursor of the modern-day Dr Shipman.

Born in Auxerre, Petiot was remembered even as a child for his sadistic and cruel nature. As a young man during the First World War he had spent his time assisting at a casualty clearing station at Dijon and lucratively engaged himself in supplying stolen morphine to drug addicts. In 1921 he qualified as a doctor and set up a practice at Villeneuve-sur-Yonne. Of a cunning nature, Petiot would often treat the poor without charge to increase his popularity and standing within the community while at the same time supplying clients with illegal drugs and carrying out illegal abortions. His murderous career may have begun early when he was suspected of causing the disappearance of his young and pregnant housekeeper, but such suspicions did not prevent a gullible community from later electing him to the post of town mayor.

Further rumours arose concerning his involvement in the deaths of two of his patients, one of whom had also been robbed. Soon after the doctor moved to Paris and set up a new practice at 60 rue de Caumartin. Outwardly he maintained a pretence of being a model citizen, a good husband and father, and he attended the local church each Sunday. His air of respectability allowed him to survive numerous accusations of being involved in drug-related offences and the mysterious disappearance of another patient.

In 1940, when the Nazi forces of occupation controlled Paris, Dr Petiot, as opportunistic as ever, devised a sinister plan for making his fortune. Simultaneously it also satisfied the perverted and sadistic propensities of his evil nature. He purchased a mansion in rue Le Sueur and installed within it a small, windowless room with one door; peepholes served as observation points into the room. A furnace was installed in the cellar beneath the garage.

Pretending to have links with the Free French, Petiot put about the rumour that he was able to smuggle hunted refugees out of France and into Spain. On making contact, potential escapees were informed that they would require expensive inoculations before being allowed to cross the border into freedom. Selling all their worldly possessions to meet Petiot's charges, they were eventually inoculated with a deadly cocktail of narcotics and then led into the tiny room, where Petiot watched them slowly die. The corpses were then treated with quicklime until they could be disposed of in the furnace.

The Gestapo, investigating the disappearance of a number of wanted Jews, became suspicious of the doctor and sent an agent posing as a refugee to the rue Le Sueur. The agent was also murdered by Petiot. The doctor was subsequently arrested by the Gestapo and detained for several months before being freed. The defence that won him his liberty was that he had the same objectives as the Nazi forces: killing Jews and anti-Nazis. Petiot was again free to continue with his evil plans.

On 11 March 1944 firemen and gendarmes were called to the rue Le Sueur because acrid smoke was billowing from a chimney. Petiot himself was absent, attending his other practice at rue de Caumartin. The gendarmes went to interview the doctor while the firemen gained entry to investigate. They were appalled to discover within the remains of twenty-seven dismembered bodies. Petiot's sly nature enabled him to escape, but he foolishly enlisted in the Free French forces under an alias.

A year later, marching down the Champs-Elysées in a victory parade, Private Petiot was recognised and apprehended. At his trial it was discovered that he had stolen from his many victims the equivalent of more than one million pounds. In the course of his trial the jury visited his execution chamber and cellar, and he was duly found guilty and sentenced to death by the Tribunal. In all, it was suspected that Petiot had murdered between sixty and seventy people, perhaps even more. As he was sentenced to death he threatened that he would be avenged, but by whom is unclear. On 25 May 1946 came his rendezvous with Desfourneaux and the guillotine, which duly sliced off the head of the scheming profiteer.

As for Henri Desfourneaux, the final five years of his career placed on him tremendous emotional demands, weakening his mind and spirit. Personal tragedy also struck the Desfourneaux's when his only son allegedly committed suicide! Other theories, though not proven, believe he was murdered by gangsters. A victim of the proverbial underworld. Like some of his predecessors, he was tortured by terrifying visions both in his waking and in his sleeping hours. In 1951, at the age of seventy-four, he died on the threshold of insanity. In the war years, during Henri Desfourneaux's tenure of the role of executioner, it was recorded that between 1939 and 1945 in France, 80 people had gone to the guillotine. This included the three women, the poisoner Elisabeth Ducourneau executed at Bordeaux on 8 January 1941. (She was the first woman to be executed since 1887.) Sinska Czeslawa executed at Chalon-sur-Saone on 29 June 1943 and the unfortunate Marie-Lousie Giraud.

In Europe as a whole, things were far worse. The greatesst use of the guillotine was in Germany and its annexed states where many thousand perished. Adolph Hitler further increased the carnage in 1941 by reducing the minimum age limit for execution to 14 years. Children could now be guillotined! Crimes which were punishable by death were also increased.

The Guillotine and the Executioners

While Anatole Deibler and Henri Desfourneaux were busy decapitating the convicted murderers of France, in neighbouring Germany other and newer guillotines were not short of victims. Over 140 years had passed since the Reign of Terror during the French Revolution. Now, in supposedly more enlightened times, another Reign of Terror had begun in Adolf Hitler's Nazi Germany. The victims of this new terror were the political opponents of the Nazis. In the period between 1933 and the end of the Second World War 16,000 political opponents of the Third Reich were guillotined behind prison walls, a criminal act of monumental proportions, far outstripping the number of executions carried out during the French Revolution. Adolf Hitler authorised the construction of twenty additional guillotines. Forty-five such devices may have been operational at one time in Germany, while just two machines sufficed in France. In 1944 the victims of the Nazi guillotines included petty thieves and even German citizens who had been apprehended listening to Allied radio broadcasts. To suggest openly that Hitler could not win the war also resulted in death upon the guillotine. Between 1943 and 1945 7,000 death sentences were passed. During 1940 some 900 German citizens went to the guillotine behind the prison walls. Vienna's District court in Austria ordered nearly 1,400 executions by guillotine for men and women who opposed the Nazi Regime of terror. Effectively the Nazi's use of the guillotine eclipsed that of the French Revolution's reign of terror in the city of Paris. During one eleven-hour period seventy-five executions were carried out using several guillotines at Plotzensee. The appalling slaughter unleashed by the Second World War masked the persecution of ordinary German citizens. Their fate was overshadowed by the Holocaust and the methods used to bring about the mass extermination of an entire race.

The Nazi guillotines differed in appearance from the French model. Teutonic engineering ensured that the blade fell more rapidly. The new design was a much shorter and squat-looking device, rather ugly in fact. The *bascule*'s rolling plank was dispensed with and a hand-operated gear mechanism was utilised to raise the increased mass of the blade to its summit. Once anchored, the cable automatically detached itself from the blade. Following the demise of the Nazi regime, the German executioner Johann Reichart recorded that he had personally executed by guillotine 2,876 political opponents of the Reich, the largest number of executions ever attributed to an individual executioner, all carried out in the so-called civilised 'modern age'. Following the Nuremberg war crimes trials, Reichart continued in his post of executioner and was protected against prosecution. Now his duties included the preparation of the gallows for the execution of Nazi extremists and leaders, although the executions were carried out by the indefatigable British hangman Albert Pierrepoint and the American Forces hangman John Woods.

In May 1949 capital punishment was suspended in West Berlin and was finally abolished in 1951. From the end of the war until the abolition of the German guillotine nine executions took place, though twenty-five people had been condemned to death. Two weeks before the suspension of capital punishment the 24-year-old murderer Berthold Wehmeyer was guillotined in the execution room of the prison on Lehrter Strasse.

The executioner in West Berlin was Gustav Volpel, a former army deserter who served between 1946 and 1948 and carried out forty-eight executions, most of them within the eastern Soviet-controlled section of Berlin. Executions in West Berlin were carried out by guillotine, those in East Berlin by axe. Volpel was the first executioner to stand trial, but not because of his trade. He was implicated in a series of armed robberies in 1948 and 1949. Demonstrating the importance of the executioner's role, he was granted a special leave of absence by the East Sector Court in order to carry out the executions of three condemned men in Dresden. They were beheaded using a 13lb axe. In the German tradition the executioner hid his identity behind a mask that covered his lower face and neck.

On another occasion Volpel was arrested for complicity in

an armed robbery, this time in the Western Sector, and was sentenced to seven years' imprisonment. He died two years after his release from prison, though his two accomplices were not so fortunate. Their lives were terminated in East Germany in 1950, beheaded by axe. Volpel's guillotine still exists in the bowels of a prison in the former West Berlin. He was fortunate not to end his life beneath his own blade.

By October 1952 no fewer than twenty-one countries had abolished the death penalty. In Europe these included West Germany, Belgium, Portugal, Norway, Sweden, Denmark, Finland, Switzerland and Italy. In France as in Britain, however, the executioner was still in employment. On 8 November 1951 a small announcement was made in *Le Figaro*: 'The new Monsieur de Paris has been designated but presently remains unknown. As is customary the name of the new executioner will not be made public until such time as an execution is to take place.'

The new executioner was André Obrecht, appointed officially as the Grand High Executioner of the Fifth Republic. There were over four hundred applicants for the post, but Obrecht's pedigree no doubt convinced the authorities that he was the right man for the job. He was fifty-two years of age and after ratification of his appointment would remain in the service of the Fifth Republic for twenty-four years, carrying out sixty-four executions as Chief Executioner.

André was the son of Jean-Baptiste Obrecht, a tailor, and Juliette Rogis. His aunt Rosalie was the wife of Anatole Deibler. As the nephew of the great Anatole he was also connected to the Rasseneux and Desfourneaux families, and was also linked with the Sansons. It was an unbeatable curriculum vitae. Like all new appointments to the prime post of chief executioner, André was no novice. He had served as an assistant under Anatole Deibler and Henri Desforuneaux his cousin's husband and had been well schooled in the art of his profession.

The common prejudice against the executing fraternity still prevailed and prevented André from marrying outside the network of families associated with the guillotine. Once again a prospective father-in-law refused to allow the union to proceed. The philanthropic father of André's bride-to-be was a committed abolitionist of capital punishment. Even André's logical approach to his prospective father-in-law could not influence the man's decision. André wrote to him:

> You are opposed to capital punishment and you make this clear by refusing your daughter's hand to an executioner. It is a point of view. But if you were to come home one night and find your wife murdered, your daughter strangled and the murderer still in the house and about to escape, what would you do? You have a gun in your pocket, will you fire or not?
>
> If you accept this act of private justice, how can you not accept what I do on behalf of legal justice? I punish criminals. I frighten off those tempted to become criminals, but I have the support of a court and I only punish murderers.

André's strong words exposed the other man's hypocrisy. Unfortunately his logical assessment had no effect and he was obliged to look elsewhere for a wife. The stigma of the guillotine again prevailed over its dutiful servant. Like many past executioners Obrecht instigated some personal changes to the guillotine. He widened the blade by welding to it an extra piece of steel. Also the metal braces that supported the structure were lightened in weight by having holes drilled through them similar in appearance to dexion. The machine also reverted to a dark red colour. Most appropriate like ox blood! It was somewhat of a strange tradition that chief executioners always seemed to want to stamp their own mark of authority onto the machine. Some satirists and traditionalists abhor these actions and liken such activities to a dog marking its territory.

By the 1950s the death sentence was reserved for the crimes of assassination, murder, poisoning, parricide and arson (presumably arson that resulted in fatality). Crimes against the state – espionage, treason, passing information to an enemy and inciting civil war – were also subject to capital punishment.

Generally speaking, those who were fed to the guillotine were usually found guilty of the most heinous of crimes.

On 16 December 1967 Gunther Volz was guillotined at Metz for rape and murder. President de Gaulle did not commute the sentence. Likewise in 1969 the abominable Jean Olivier was sentenced to death for the murder of two children aged ten and twelve, one of the children having been raped. The president again withheld his prerogative and Olivier was duly guillotined early in the morning of 11 March at Amiens. Perhaps General de Gaulle empathised with the sentiments of Jean-Jacques Rousseau:

When such a crime is perpetrated against an innocent individual, who is naturally and rightly so protected under the ambit of authority of the state, then the violator of the crime has waived his right to the protection of the state. His social rights so cruelly denied to his victim become forfeit. The preservation of the state is inconsistent with his own and one or the other must perish.

The guillotine does not slay the citizen, but rather the enemy.

With fewer executions now taking place, the job of the executioner became a part-time one. Whenever it was necessary, the guillotine would be transported to a provincial prison in a small covered van and assembled behind the prison walls. The execution would be carried out diligently and quietly, before the machine was dismantled and transported back to Paris and the Santé prison. Executions were only briefly reported in the newspapers; indeed, for all practical purposes the machine had disappeared. It might even have come as a surprise to the less well-informed young Frenchman that the guillotine was still in use. With pressure mounting from the European Community and the internal opponents of capital punishment, it was reasonable to assume that the guillotine would soon become part of history.

By 1973 more than forty countries had abolished the death penalty, but an opinion poll in France suggested that the French still remained in favour of capital punishment. The British government had effectively abolished hanging in 1964. The last man condemned to hang smiled after the judge had donned his black cap and spoken the words of the death sentence. Ronald Cooper had been found guilty of the capital crime of murder, having killed an elderly company director. But it had already been leaked to the media that the Home Secretary would reprieve all those convicted of murder until the Abolition of the Death Penalty Bill had been debated in Parliament. This was effectively the end of hanging in Britain.

President Pompidou took office in France in 1969 after the guillotining of the child murderer and rapist Olivier. He stated openly that for as long as he was president there would be no further executions. Between 1969 and 1973 President Pompidou spared 12 potential victims from death upon the guillotine. It looked as if André Obrecht, now aged seventy-one, was becoming redundant. He was not! President Pompidou was unable to keep his promise. On 12 May 1973 André Obrecht guillotined the Tunisian Ali Ben Yanès, aged thirty-four, who had murdered a little girl of seven. President Valery Giscard d'Estaing seemed to place more emphasis on the upholding of the tradition of French justice and retribution by authorising three executions between 1976 and 1977. On 28 July 1976 Christian Ranucci was guillotined at Marseille. It was Obrecht's last execution. He was seventy-six years old. He lived on, but died of Parkinson's disease in 1985.

André Obrecht was replaced by France's last executioner Marcel Chevalier. As chief executioner he would only be called upon twice to carry out the last executions before the abandonment of capital punishment.

Chevalier was married to André Obtrecht's niece and had assisted previously at forty executions. He had officially been appointed an aide in 1958 along with fellow recruit Raymond Navarre.

At the young age of fifty-five he was now chief executioner, appointed from 1 October 1976. Under Chevalier's supervision, the guillotine went to Douai on 23 June 1977 to despatch Jerôme Carrein. It's pentultimate victim.

The Guillotine and the Executioners

The final execution took place at Marseille inside Les Baumettes prison at 4.40 a.m. on 10 September 1977. Hamida Djandoubi was a Tunisian immigrant that had been living and working in Marseilles from 1968. A workplace accident ended with him losing two thirds of his right leg. It was an ironic twist of fate that he would also eventually lose his heead.

During 1973, twenty-one year old Elisabeth Bousquet complained to the authorities that Djanboubi had held her against her will and subjected her to cruelty. Following his arrest and eventual release from custody he became involved with two young girls and forced them to 'work' for him but his ambition was to seek revenge on Bousquet and in July 1974 he kidnapped her and took her to his home. In front of the two young girls Djanboubi beat Bousquet without mercy increasing her agony by stubbing lighted cigarette ends over her breasts and genital areas. He then took her to the outskirts of Marseilles and strangled her.

Her body was found in a shed by two young children and formally identified a month later. It was after this that the two girls who had witnessed the torture of Busoquet went to the police. At the court in Aix-en-Provence he was accused of premeditated violence, torture, rape and murder.

He argued that his conduct was the result of the amputation of his leg that had driven him towards alcohol and violence but this defence was not acceptable and on the 25 February he was sentenced to death. His appeal for presidential grace was refused and early in the morning of 10 September, Chevalier and his assistants quietly assembled the guillotine. Unknown to them it would be for the last time.

The last man condemned to death by guillotine was Phillipe Maurice. He was offered Presidential grace on 25 May 1981. Today he is a free man and a citizen of good standing. While in prison he began to study history and in 1995 qualified for his doctorate. He speicalises in medieval history.

As for the guillotine, in 1971 Jacques Lerouge who spent three months in the condemned cell once said, 'We do not call it by that name, guillotine! It is known as the widow, for that is its function . . . It makes widows!' He was eventually freed from prison in 1992.

After October 1981 all of those condemned to death were automatically pardoned and their sentences altered to life imprisonment. Had it been different, Chevalier and his guillotine were due to visit a further six towns. It did not transpire. The executioner's unique vocation in the great scheme of life and death was over.

In 1981 Chevalier lost his part-time executioner's job and went back to his full-time employment as a printer's assistant. The sound of the crashing blade was finally silenced.

Epilogue

The guillotine was born amidst the violence and turmoil of the French Revolution. This began as a humanitarian movement characterised by enlightenment, and the machine itself was developed by two men of science motivated by the concepts of justice and human rights. Those who steered the Revolution on its erratic course were men of discernment, determined to exercise their particular role in developing the kind of society they envisaged. Such a society would have at its heart the concept of justice, and not revenge. Thus the guillotine became the Timbers of Justice.

It is hard for us to see this philanthropic motive, this concern for justice and equality, when we think of the relentless fall of the blade. But at the time the guillotine seemed the last word in surgical precision and painless efficiency. Indeed, as an instrument of capital punishment the guillotine has probably never been surpassed, decapitation taking place in a fraction of a second. In terms of the culture of punishment, the guillotine brought an end, at least initially, to the gruesome public spectacle of slow and uncertain death at the hands of the executioner. The machine became the executioner; human involvement was reduced to the barest minimum.

The simplicity and efficiency of this technical, scientific and thoroughly modern device made it a particularly frightening tool in the hands of tyrannical governments. This was the case in the French Revolution, when the sheer efficiency of the 'National Razor' meant that political execution could be achieved in large numbers and with little adverse reaction from the people. It is widely accepted that if execution with the sword had still been the custom, the people would never have stood for such large-scale judicial murder. The swift, sure blade of the Timbers of Justice gave – to the observer at least – the impression of impersonal, scientific dispatch. In propaganda terms the guillotine was a great success.

Its value as a tool of political propaganda meant that executions in France remained as public as they had ever been. The guillotine acquired a dramatic, ritual force, and death on the high scaffold was a powerful symbol of government strength, particularly during the later years of the nineteenth century when anarchy threatened the stability of France. Once again the guillotine was used to remove political enemies of the state.

Changing attitudes to crime and punishment meant that by the late twentieth century, somewhat later than in other western countries, the death penalty was abolished in France. So strong was the government's opposition to it, and to the very idea of the guillotine, that during the celebrations marking the bicentenary of the Revolution, eight years after it had officially been abandoned, it was forbidden to use images of the guillotine. The association of the Timbers of Justice with the high ideals of the Revolution was thus officially denied.

The inglorious career of the guillotine technically and for all practical purposes ended in September 1977, the last time it was used in an execution. It was apparent that the dread machine that had helped shape a modern nation had at last outlived its usefulness. Though there has been no serious public demand for its reinstatement, its impact on the methods and the morality of capital punishment is still felt. The fact that the last victims of the guillotine were from ethnic or other minority groups was a further element in its discrediting. The weakest and most vulnerable members of society enjoyed the *toilette du condamné*, while those with better connections avoided it. What could be more unfair, unscientific, inhumane?

But despite the modern revulsion for the guillotine, its fascination allows it to live on in the arts, theatre and cinema. Whenever it appears, it still retains the power to dominate the imagination. The present home of the real guillotine is in

Epilogue

Le Musée National des Prisons. Before this is 1981, it was located at the Fresnes prison. Now a quarter of a century later, it still remains hidden from public view. The pariah of state vengeance remains behind closed doors, probably in a disassembled state, and is not available for public scrutiny or study. The late André Obrecht, former Chief Executioner of the Fifth Republic, felt that he had been a useful citizen and spoke with pride:

> Capital punishment has been abolished but that does not mean it will not be brought back again one day in the future. When murderers having been allowed to live for too long spread their evil and darkness over our world, then the people will wish to re-establish the inexorable light. It is not in vain that I have been the representative of many centuries of human order.

The blade of the guillotine may now no longer fall, but, as the saying has it, you can never say never! In 1995 a Democrat from the state of Georgia in the USA proposed a bill to replace the state's electric chair with a guillotine:

> The General Assembly finds that while a prisoner condemned to death may wish to donate one or more of their organs for transplant, any such desire is thwarted by the fact that electrocution makes all such organs unsuitable for transplant . . . All persons who have been convicted of a capital offence and have imposed upon them a sentence of death shall, at the election of the condemned, suffer such punishment either by electrocution or the guillotine . . .

His proposal was not accepted, but it makes a fascinating epitaph for the humane and enlightened views of the good Dr Guillotin.

The Revolutionary Calendar

Revolutionary Month	Year Two of the Republic
1 Vendémiaire	22 September 1793
10	1 October 1793
20	11
1 Brumaire	22
10	31
20	10 November 1793
1 Frimaire	21
10	30
20	10 December 1793
1 Nivôse	21
10	30
20	9 January 1794
1 Pluviôse	20
10	29
20	8 February 1794
1 Ventôse	19
10	28
20	10 March 1794
1 Germinal	21
10	30
20	9 April 1794
1 Floréal	20
10	29
20	9 May 1794
1 Prairial	20
10	29
20	8 June 1794

The Revolutionary Calendar

1 Messidor	19
10	28
20	8 July 1794
1 Thermidor	19
10	28
20	7 August 1794
1 Fructidor	18
10	27
20	6 September 1794

The revolutionary Calendar, devised by Fabre d'Eglantine, was introduced on 22 September 1793 to celebrate the anniversary of the declaration of the First Republic. In accordance with the revolutionary virtues of reason and nature, the calendar divided the year into twelve thirty-day months, named after their appropriate seasons. The five outstanding days, the *sans-culottides*, were later named 'contemporary' days. The Calendar remained in use until 1806.

Appendix 1

THE PAY OF THE EXECUTIONER

Before the Revolution executioners were granted the right of havage, whereby they were entitled to take a toll of corn, fruit and other consumables sold in the markets. It was also usual for the executioner to be a 'slaughterman', usually the town's 'knacker', and he was allowed to sell for his own profit the procurements from the dead animals. Home-made medicinal remedies and ointments were also sold for a variety of common ailments. The right of havage provided for a substantial income of 60,000 livres a year when added to an annual salary of 6,000 livres. In 1775 the ancient right of havage was withdrawn, except for some minor privileges, greatly reducing the income of the executioners, particularly those in provincial France. In general the pay scales for the executioners followed these guidelines:

Annual Pay Scales

Revolutionary Period

Paris executioner	10,000 livres
Town of population 100,000–300,000	6,000 livres
Town of population 50,000–100,000	4,000 livres
Town of population less than 50,000	2,400 livres

Post-Revolutionary Period

Paris executioner, *c.* 1832	8,000 francs
Lyons	5,000 francs
Bordeaux	4,000 francs
Provincial executioners	2,000–5,000 francs
Towns of population less than 20,000	2,000 francs

Appendix 1

Later Salaries

Paris executioner in 1849	5,000 francs
National executioner in 1870	6,000 francs
Two assistants to the national executioner	4,000 francs
Three assistants to the national executioner	3,000 francs
National executioner in 1939	10,000 francs
Last appointed full-time executioner	60,000 francs

Note: Monetary values: one livre = approximately one franc
Approximately 10 francs = one pound sterling (1999)

In 1906 all allowances were withdrawn, though they were later reinstated. The upkeep and maintenance of the guillotine and travelling costs were made the responsibility of the chief executioner. This was a political initiative by the abolitionists. The reinstatement of emoluments granted the executioner and his assistants free travel while on official business, plus a travel allowance of 8 francs per day.

Appendix 2

THE EXECUTIONERS OF PARIS

Charles-Henri Sanson	1778–95
Henri Sanson	1795–1840
Clément-Henri Sanson	1840–47
Charles André Férey	1847–49
Jean-François Heindreicht	1849–72
Nicolas Roch	1872–79
Louis Deibler	1879–99
Anatole Deibler	1899–1939
Jules-Henri Desfourneaux	1939–51
André Obrecht	1951–76
Marcel Chevalier	1976–81

Appendix 3

LOCATIONS OF THE PARIS GUILLOTINE

Place de Grève	April 1792	First use, Pelletier executed
Place du Carrousel	August 1792– December 1792	Political offenders executed
Place de Grève	August 1792– December 1792	Common law offenders executed
Place de la Révolution	January 1793	Sited between the remains of Louis XV statue and the entrance to the Champs-Elysées. Site of execution of Louis XVI
Place du Carrousel	May 1793	Thought to be too close to the Convention so removed
Place de la Révolution	May 1793	Between the pedestal and the garden of the Tuileries. Phase 1 of the Terror. Situated here for thirteen months
Place du Trône	June 1794	Phase 2 of the Terror. Situated here for six weeks

Place de Grève	June 1794	A second scaffold erected for common law offenders
Place de la Révolution	July 1794	Execution of Robespierre. Three hundred executions in three days
Place de Grève	July 1794	Tinville, public prosecutor, executed
Place de la Révolution	May 1795	
Place de Grève	Post-Revolutionary period	Traditionally the square where executions took place
Place Saint-Jacques	1832–1851	
Place de la Roquette	1851–1899	Near the prison
Boulevard Arago	1899–1939	Outside the wall of La Santé Prison
La Santé prison	1939–1977	In a courtyard within the prison

Appendix 4

MARIE-ANTOINETTE'S LAST LETTER

The words inscribed on Marie-Antoinette's statue were written on the morning of her death, 16 October 1793, in her cell in the Conciergerie. The letter was addressed to Madame Elisabeth, the king's sister, who had charge of her children. The queen had doubts that the letter would ever reach her sister-in-law: her fears were well founded.

4.30 a.m. 16 October
It is to you Sister that I am writing for the last time. I have just been sentenced to death, but not to a shameful one, since this death is shameful only to criminals, whereas I am going to rejoin your brother. Innocent like him, I hope to show the firmness which he showed during his last moments. I am calm as one may well be when one's conscience is clear, though I am deeply grieved at having to forsake my poor children. My good and affectionate Sister, you know that I only existed for them and for you who in the kindness of your heart sacrificed everything in order to be with us – in what a terrible position do I leave you! It was during the trial that I learned my daughter had been separated from you. Alas, poor child, I do not dare write to her, for I know she would not receive my letter. I do not even know if this letter will reach you. However, through you I send them both my blessing hoping that one day when they are older, they will be with you once more and enjoy your tender care. If only they will both continue to think the thoughts with which I have never ceased to inspire them,

namely that sound principles and the exact performance of duties are the prime foundation of life, and that mutual love and confidence will bring them happiness. . . . They should learn from our example, how much consolation we had from our affection for each other despite all misfortunes, and how sharing happiness with a friend redoubles it and where can one find a more affectionate, more loving friend than in one's own family? I hope my son will always remember his father's last words, which I repeat – Let him never try to avenge our deaths. I must say something about my son which is extremely painful. I know how much my little boy must have hurt you [untrue accusations of incest inspired by vindictive revolutionaries]. Forgive him dear sister, remember how young he is and how easy it is to make a child say whatever one wants especially when he does not understand. I hope the day will come when he will realise the full value of your kindness and affection you have shown to both of my children.

All that now remains is to tell you of my last thoughts. I should have liked to write them before the trial opened, but apart from the fact that I was not allowed to write, things have moved so quickly that I really have not had the time.

I die in the Catholic, Apostolic and Roman religion, in the faith of my father in which I was brought up and which I have always professed. I have no hope of any spiritual consolation, not even aware whether there are still priests of this faith in France. I believe that even if they are it would be far too dangerous for them to visit me. I sincerely ask for God's forgiveness for all the faults I have committed since I was born. I trust that in His goodness, He will hear my final prayers, as well as those that I have long been making and that in His pity and His goodness, He may receive my soul.

I ask the forgiveness of all those whom I have known and especially of my sister, for the sorrow which unwittingly, I may have caused you. I forgive my enemies the evil they have done me. I bid farewell to my aunts and to my brothers and sisters. Once I had friends too. The thought of my separation from them for ever and of their worries is among my greatest regrets in dying. Do let them know that they were in my thoughts until the last moments of my life.

Farewell my good and loving sister. I only hope that this letter will reach you. Always think of me. I send you my most heartfelt love and send it as well to my poor dear children. My God, it is agony to leave them forever. Goodbye, goodbye. Now I must attend to my spiritual duties. Perhaps they will bring me a priest of their own since I am a prisoner. I declare however that I shall not say a word to him and will treat him as a total stranger.

When she had finished the letter, she lay down and wept. Later she also wrote a brief note to her children. 'Oh, my God, have pity on me! My eyes have no tears left to weep for you, my poor children. Goodbye! Goodbye!'

Neither letter was delivered. Madame Elisabeth was herself guillotined on 10 May 1794. The queen's infant son, Louis XVII, now deformed, died in the Temple prison in June 1795, his spirit broken, degraded by illness and vile treatment. Her daughter, Madame Royale, eventually the Duchesse d'Angoulême, was given over to the Austrians in exchange for French soldiers held captive. She died in 1851.

Bibliography

PUBLISHED WORKS

Badinter, R., *The Execution* (Paris, Bernard Grasset, 1973)

Belbenoit, R., *Dry Guillotine* (E.P. Dutton & Co. Inc., from the original translation from the French by Preston Rambo, 1938)

Belloc, H., *Life of Danton* (Thomas Nelson & Sons, n.d.)

Bressler, F., *Reprieve* (Harrop, 1965)

Byron, George Gordon, Lord, *Selected Letters and Journals* (ed. Leslie A. Marchand, 1982)

Carlyle, T., *The French Revolution, a History* (1837)

Chapman, P., *Madame Tussaud's Chamber of Horrors* (Constable, 1984)

Cronin, V., *Louis and Antoinette* (Purnell Book Services, 1974)

Dickens, C., *A Tale of Two Cities* (1859)

——, 'A Public Execution', in *Dickens in Europe* (ed. Rosalind Vallence, 1975)

Doyle, W., *Oxford Dictionary of the French Revolution* (Oxford University Press, 1989)

Du Bois, L., *Recherches historiques et physiologiques sur la guillotine* (1843) (Paris, Chez France)

Edgeworth, Abbé, *Memoirs of the Abbé Edgeworth, Containing his Narrative of the Last Hours of Louis XVI* (1815)

Elliot, J., *The Way of the Tumbrils* (Max Reinhardt Ltd, 1958)

Fleischmann, H., *The Guillotine in 1793* (Librairie des Publications Modernes, Paris, 1908)

Gerould, D., *Guillotine – Its Legend and Lore* (Blast Books, NY, 1992)

Kershaw, A., *History of the Guillotine* (Calder Publishing, 1958)

Bibliography

Lenotre, G., *The Guillotine and its Servants* (Hutchinson & Co. Ltd, trans. Rodolph Stawell, n.d.)

Levy, B., *Legacy of Death* (Saxon House D.C. Heath Ltd, 1973)

Sanson, Henri-Clément, *Executioners All. Memoirs of the Sanson Family from private notes and documents 1688–1847*. Edited by Henri Sanson late executioner of the court of Justice of Paris (Neville Spearman Ltd, 1962)

Seward, D., *Marie-Antoinette* (Constable, 1981)

Shuckburgh, E., *Memoirs of Madame Roland* (Barrie & Jenkins, trans. and ed. Evelyn Shuckburgh, 1989)

Soubiran, A., *Ce Bon Docteur Guillotin* (Souvenir Press Ltd, trans. Malcolm MacCraw, 1962)

Tannahill, R., *Paris in the Revolution* (Folio Society, 1966)

Turgenev, I., *The Execution of Troppmann* (Turgenev's Literary Reminiscences, Minerva Press, 1968)

PERIODICALS AND NEWSPAPERS

Chronique de Paris
Le Figaro
Le Moniteur

Data on the French guillotine can also be found on the Jorn Fabricus's website,
http;//www.guillotine.dk

Index

Allorto, Joseph Quentin 142, 149, 150
anarchists 161–9
Anders, Alfred 172
Anderson, Gordon 152, 163
Austro–French relations 64, 69, 70
Avignon 61–2
Avril Pierre 140

Badinter, Robert 6, 8, 9, 10, 12
Barjavel 61
bascule 6, 27, 51, 72, 97, 106
Bastille 17, 20, 68, 86, 163
Beaurieux, Dr 132–3
Belgium, use of the guillotine 171
Belbenoit, René 151
Berger, Alphonse Léon 150, 171
Bicêtre hospital 42–4, 47, 53, 93, 128
blood 85–6, 88, 107, 118, 166–7
Bluebeard (Henri-Desiré Landru) 172–3
Bontemps, Roger 1–4, 7–9, 11, 12
Borel, Richard 99–100

Boulay, Lucien 173
Bousquet, Elisabeth 187
Buffet, Claude 1–4, 9, 11, 12
Byron, Lord George 63–4

Cabanis, Dr 126
Cachard 54
Cadoudal, Georges 128
capital punishment *see also* executions
    abolition 11, 136–7, 181, 182, 185–6
    equality 13, 21–2, 23–4, 53
    opposition to 10, 21, 123, 142–3
Carmelite nuns 110
Carnot, Sadi 165
Carrein, Jerôme 186
Carrera, Xavier 167
Carrichon, Abbé 74, 117–18
Carton, Sydney 62
Casério, Santo 165–6
chapiteau 152, 154
Chardon, widow 140
Chauffeur's de la Drôme 161
Chenier, André 82
Chevalier, Marcel 186, 188
Cipierre, Firmin 134–5
Clairin, architect 56

Index

Clavière, Minister of taxes 36, 39–40

Conciergerie prison, Paris 76, 79, 81, 82, 83, 87, 116

Cooper, Ronald 186

Corday, Charlotte 60, 82, 92, 115, 116, 121

corpses, disposal 108–111, 115, 118–19

Couty de la Pommerais, Guy 122–3

Creieux, Adolph 145

Crozes, Abbé 151

Cullerier, Dr Michael 43–5

Curtius, Philippe Dr 101–2

Czeslawa, Sinska 180

d'Angremont, Louis-David Collenot 54

d'Estaing, Valery Giscard 186

Damiens, François 16, 17, 80

Damoiseau 170

Danton, Georges 14, 82–3, 116, 119

de Gaulle, Charles 185

de Lignières, Dr 130–1

de Noailles, Madame le Maréchale 116–18

de Saint Victor, Coster 128

death penalty *see* capital punishment

Decaisne, E. Dr 129

Decaisne, G. Dr 129

Dehaene, Jean 176

Deibler, Anatole 107, 143, 158–9, 160, 167–9, 170–4

Deibler, Joseph 157–8

Deibler, Louis 96, 150, 153, 157–9, 160 161, 162, 163, 164, 165, 166, 167

anarchist, target 161–6

Desbrosses 54

Descolozeaux 113–4

Desfourneaux, Jules Henri 171, 174–5, 176, 177, 178, 180, 181

Djandoubi, Hamida 187

Deroo, Théophile 160

Desmoulins, Camille 82, 119

Devils Island (film) 161

Devils Island, French Guiana 94, 161

Devitre 54

Dickens, Charles 17, 62–3

du Barry, Madame Marie Jeanne 82, 89–90, 116, 139

Dubois 95–6

Ducourneau, Elisabeth 180

Dumas, Alexandre 42, 46, 100

Duval, G. 121–2

Edgeworth de Firmont, Abbé 70–1, 73

Elisabeth, Princess 82, 101, 102, 115, 116

Erler, Fritz 135

Errancis cemetery, Paris 112, 119

executioners
    dynasties 150, 156–9, 168, 169, 183
    public's attitude to, 138,

141–2, 143–4, 161–2,
168–70, 183–4
executions *see also* capital
punishment; guillotine
blood produced, 85–6,
88–7, 108, 109, 118,
166–7
decapitation favoured 21,
22–5, 27–8
descriptions 6–10, 86,
106–7, 118
filming 160–1, 175
first use of the guillotine
49–53
Louis XVI 64–5, 70–2,
73–5, 83
Marie Antoinette 73, 75–8
medical controvery 120–1,
123–7, 135–7
medical experiments 121–4,
126–33, 136–7
pre guillotine methods
15–17, 25–7, 28, 30,
32–5
public 4–5, 49–53, 86–90,
149–150, 170–1
victims' routes 83–5, 87–8
witnesses 5, 62–4, 121–2,
146–7, 170

Fallières, Armand 142–3
Férey, Charles André 145,
156
Festival of the Supreme Being
88, 109,
Fiesch, Margot 166
Fouquier Tinville, Principal

Prosecuter 76, 77, 81–2,
86, 102, 115
Fournier, Etienne 136
Frederick III prince de Salm
Kilburg 119
French Guiana 94, 104, 161
French Revolution 13–14 *see
also* Reign of Terror
origins 17–19, 66–70
outbreak 20, 68–70
provinces 103–6
religion 85, 110–11

Garnatel, Marcel 135
Gautier, Dr Pierre 124, 125
Germany
occupation of France
176–80
use of guillotine 124, 171,
181–3
Giraud, architect 55
Giraud, Marie-Louise 178,
180
Girondin faction 60, 64–5, 82,
91
Guedon, builder 50, 56, 57
first guillotine 36–42
Guillotin, Dr Joseph-Ignace
advocating decapitation
21–3, 35
birth 15, 17
early career 18–19
goes into hiding 60–1
later life 61
name linked to the
guillotine 35–6, 47–8,
54, 61

Index

penal code reform 21–5, 28
testing the first guillotine 43–6
guillotine *see also* executions
  blade 46–7, 93–4, 107, 108, 145, 151–3
  conducted tours 96–7, 146–7
  descriptions 6, 26–7, 94, 106–7, 153–5
  Dr Louis specifications 32–5, 36–7
  first machine 35–6, 40–2, 94–6, 100
  German version 124, 171, 181–3
  last use 11–12, 137, 188, 190
  locations 86–9, 94–5, 121–2,
  Madame Tussaud's waxworks 100–1, 102–3
  modifications 45, 46, 47, 94, 107, 139, 145–6, 151–3
  nicknames 4, 54, 108, 189
  outside France 62–4, 124, 171–2, 181–3, 191
  precursors 26–7, 35–7
  proliferation 61–2, 93–4
  proposed 22–5,
  Reign of Terror, facilitating 59, 79, 85–6, 138–9, 189–90
  testing 42–8
  variations 93, 106, 181–2

Halifax Gibbet 26, 35

Harsch, Dominique 166
Hébert, Jacques 102, 116
Heindreicht, Jean-François 96, 145, 148, 150–1, 156
Henry, Emile 164
Hespel (the jackal) 94, 104–5
Hitler, Adolf 124, 172, 181
Hoang Kha 172
Hugo, Victor 12, 97

Italy, use of the guillotine 62–3

Jacobin faction 59–60, 64–5, 91–2
Jenner, Edward 61

Karloff, Boris 161
Koenigstein, François Claudius (Ravachol) 162–3, 164

La Santé prison, Paris 1, 3, 4, 174
Lacenaire, Pierre-François 128, 140, 145
Lacombe 106
Lacretelle, Dr 44
Lafayette, General of the National Guard 50, 67
Landru, Henri–Désiré (Bluebeard) 172–3
Langer, Marcel 177
Languille, Henri 131
Lanz, Pierre 160
Lavoisier, Antoine 82
Leclerc, Anne 54

Lefevre, Louis 155
le Gros, François 121
Lerouge, Jaques 187
Leveille, J.B. Dr 126
Leveling 127
Lignierès, Dr Dassy de 130–1
Lothringer, Abbé 77
Louis XV 16
Louis XVI 13, 28
    arrest 68–70
    burial 111, 113
    death-mask 102
    execution 64–5, 70–2, 83
    modifications to guillotine
        42, 46–7
    reign 66–8
Louis, Dr Antoine
    first guillotine 35, 36–8,
        42–6
    guillotine, disociates
        himself 35, 48, 54–5
    guillotine specifications
        32–5, 36–7
Louisette' 35, 38
Louivion, J.B 93
lunette 27, 97, 106, 107, 151,
    152
Lux, Adam 116

Madame Tussaud's waxworks
    100, 102–3
Madeleine cemetery, Paris
    109–10, 113–4, 115, 116
Maiden, The 26–27
Marat, Jean-Paul 60, 75, 82,
    92, 102
Maret, Dr 44

Marie-Antoinette 13, 66
    arrest 68–9
    burial 113–4
    death-mask 102
    execution 73, 76–8
    trial 75, 76
Marignan, Madame 95
Martin, Georges 133–5, 177
Martin, Robert 177
Maurice, Philippe 187
medical controversy 120–1,
    123–6, 132–7
medical experiments 121–4,
    126–33, 135–7
Ménesclou, Louis 130–1
Mercier, Louis-Sébastien 72
Meyssonnier, Fernand 152, 163
Mirabeau, Compte de 69
Moniteur, Le 125, 126
Monsieur de Paris' 99, 150,
    156, 183
Mory, Carmen 176
mouton 106, 107, 151–2, 153

Napoleon I 113, 128, 157
National Assembly creation 68
    Dr Louis' report 32–5
    French penal code reform
        20–5, 27–8
    introduction of guillotine
        31–2
    Jacobin dominance 59–60,
        91–2
National Convention 64–5
Navarre, Raymond 186
Necker, Jacques 67
Nysten, Dr 44

Index

Obrecht, André 175, 183–4, 186

Olivier, Jean 185

O'Mahony, Count 95

Paris, Madame 119–9

Paris Universal Exposition 149

Pelletier, Nicolas-Jacques 31, 36, 41, 49–52

Petiot, Dr Marcel 178–80

Pettigand, Dr 132–3

Philipon, Manon 115

Philippe Egalité 74, 82, 116

'photographer' 155–56

Picpus cemetery, Paris 109, 112, 116, 119

Piedelievre, R. Dr 136

Pierrepoint, Albert 142, 182

Pilorges, Maurice 174

Pinal, Dr 44

Place de Grève 49, 51, 86

Place de la Révolution 64, 79, 83, 85, 87, 88, 108–9

Place de Roquette 122, 147, 178

Place du Carrousel 54, 87, 94

Place du Trône 88, 109, 116, 117, 118, 119

Place St-Jacques 140

Pollet brothers 159, 160

Pommerais, Guy 122–3

Pompidou, Georges 2, 3, 143, 186

Prunier, Théotime 129–30

Prussia, war against France 69–70

Peugnez, Alfred 170

quai de la Megisserie 79, 84

quai de l'Horloge 79, 83

Question, The 15, 16, 28

Rakida, Abdelkader 174

Ranucci, Christian 186

Rasseneux, Antoine 158

Ravachol see Koenigstein, François Claudius

Reichart, Johann 182

Reign of Terror 13–14, 65, 89, 103–4, 109–10

see also French Revolution

guillotine facilitates 59, 79, 85, 138, 189–90

religion, French Revolution 85, 110

Revolutionary Tribunal 75, 76, 80–1, 87–8, 103–4

death toll 110, 117, 118–9

Robespierre, Maximilien 21, 65, 82, 84, 91, 115, 119

execution 60–1, 82, 102

Roch, Nicolas 95, 150–2, 153, 159

Roederer, Procureur General 50, 55, 56, 57, 58

first guillotine 35–6, 38–41

Rogis, Louis 173

Rogis, Rosalie 168

Roland, Madame 82, 84, 115

Rykerwaert, Rachael 171

Saint-Just, Louis 82, 86, 102, 119

Sanson, Charles-Henri 24,
    29–31, 124
  execution of Louis XVI 64–5
  execution of Marie-
    Antoinette 76–8
  first execution with
    guillotine 51–2
  first guillotine built 39–40,
    44, 45, 46, 47
  Reign of Terror 79, 81,
    82–5, 88–90, 108–9,
    115–6
Sanson, Clément–Henri 47,
    140–1, 145, 156
  disgraced 98–100, 103
  guillotine guided tours
    96–7, 98
Sanson, Gabriel 86
Sanson, Henri 93, 138, 145
  execution of Louis XVI
    73–4,
  execution of Marie
    Antoinettte 73, 76–7, 78
  guillotine guided tours
    96–7
Sardou, Victorien 147, 148
Scarlet Pimpernel, The 161
Schmidt, Tobias 41–2, 45,
    55–9
Sedillot, Dr 125
Seguret, Dr 143
Sellier, Jean Baptiste Désiré
    142, 149, 150
Solleilland 143
Soemmering, Dr Samuel
    124–6
Sue, Jean-Joseph Dr 122

Tale of Two Cities, A 17, 62
Terrier 127
Thermomètre du Jour 71, 73
Thomas Cook & Co. 149
toilette du condamné 7, 8, 81,
    97, 148, 190
Tragedies of 1793, The 42, 46
tricoteuses 81
Troppmann, Jean–Baptiste
    146–9
Tuileries palace of 68, 78, 108
Tussaud Joseph 96, 100
Tussaud, Madame Marie
    100–3

Vacher, Joseph 173
Vaillant, Auguste 163, 164
Valazé, Charles 91
Vaujour, Colonel 90
Velpea, Dr 122–3
Victims' Balls 92
Villiers de L'Isle-Adam, Comte
    de 122–3
Volpel, Gustav 182–3
Voltz, Gunther 185
Vromant, Canut 160

waxworks, Madame Tussaud's
    182–3
Wedekind, Dr 126
Weidmann, Eugène 174–6
Woods, John 182

Yanès, Ali Ben 186

Zuckermeyer, Aloïs 171